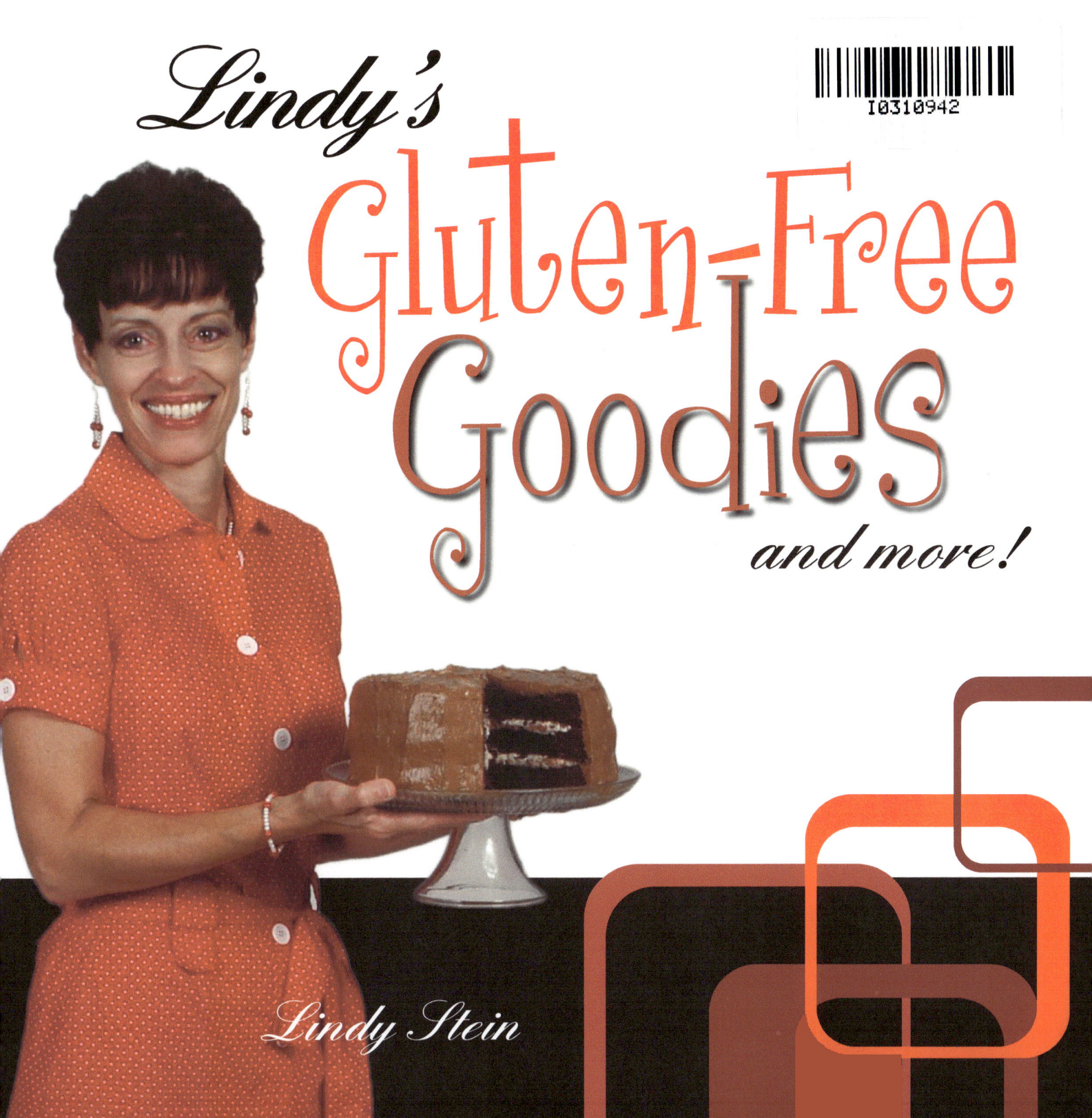

Copyright © 2012-Present Lindy Stein

Visit Lindy online at www.LindysLessons.com

All rights reserved. No part of this publication may be reproduced or transmitted in any form or by any means, including informational storage and retrieval systems, without permission in writing from the copyright holder, except for brief quotations in a review.

This book's content is for informational purposes only and is not intended to replace professional nutritional or medical advice.

Cover and Interior Design by Kristen Joy
Published by Tintrí Press
Green Bay, WI

ISBN 13: 978-0-9852577-3-6

Third Tintrí Press printing, October 2016

Dedication

To my daughter who has been an amazing source of support and encouragement and the BEST book publishing coach there is!

To my Lord and Savior, Jesus Christ who gave me the desire and talent to bake, cook and serve others with my endeavors.

Acknowledgements

Thanks to:

Rhoda Hochstetler and Ann Holden, owners of Curves in Plain City, who allowed me to provide taste-tests to the many Curves members.

All the Curves of Plain City members for the encouragement and willingness to be my guinea pigs.

All the families of *Lindy's Lessons Studio* who eagerly participated in the endless taste testing.

Monica Carter for her support, encouragement and help in guiding me through the first few months in the gluten-free world.

Introduction

It was in February of 2008 that a saliva test revealed that I was allergic to eggs, wheat, dairy and soy. The news was difficult. I love to bake and cook. Now I was faced with trying to find a way to do something I enjoy with extreme limitations. The doctor told me to fast from one food group at a time. The easiest was to give up eggs. I replaced eggs with Ener-g Egg Replacer. This worked well for most of my recipes. My doctor asked me if I noticed any difference in how I felt. I said, "not really." Then he asked do you feel any different emotionally. I really did not, but it did make me realize that foods do affect our bodies and emotions.

The history of problem foods in my immediate family goes back to when my daughter was very small. Her first allergy to foods was discovered after I fed her a pecan shortbread cookie. The reaction was a horrible rash all over her body. This little one-year-old literally scratched herself raw from the itch. We learned that by putting a small portion of suspected foods on her skin we could test food allergies. We found she was allergic to all nuts except peanuts.

At about 10 years old she was skin tested for 24 allergies that were not food related. She was allergic to 20 things. I washed her bedclothes every week. I put plastic covers on her mattress to keep the dust mite feces away from her. Holidays were very difficult because of all her allergies. The added excitement of those special days caused her to lose sleep and that made her more susceptible to bronchitis and other diseases.

I later learned that she was allergic to MSG (monosodium glutamate). This flavor enhancer is in so many restaurant foods that it is difficult to find a place that does not use it. When she was little she would complain that her stomach hurt after eating. It seemed like nothing she ate in a restaurant was pleasing to her except macaroni and cheese. It wasn't until her freshman year in college that I found MSG to be a major factor in her stomach problems. To this day she can literally pass out from one bite of food that contains it.

Now let me tell you about my wheat problem. After being off the eggs for 2 months I removed wheat from my diet. I began my research first in baking gluten-free breads. I bought several books by Bette Hagman. She was known as the gluten-free gourmet. I tried several of her bread recipes and with a little more of my own experimenting came up with the right proportions of the ingredients that worked for me. It was especially hard to get the bread to rise and stay risen. I am a perfectionist. When I read a recipe I follow it to the letter. I hate to experiment. But since this gluten-free, wheat free issue was essential for me to know how wheat was affecting me, I had to do it. With the minor adjustments to her bread recipes my bread now rises quite nicely.

While I was working on all this bread baking I began to hear stories from my clients and doctor about people who had celiac disease. This disease comes as a result of being gluten intolerant. It may not show itself at first but over time a person who has celiac disease will gradually feel run down and depressed. This disease if not stopped can lead to cancer and other life-threatening diseases.

Gluten affects a person with celiac disease by literally rubbing the villi (the tiny hair-like stems in the small intestine that collect nutrients) raw. Gluten acts like sand paper on the villi. With the villi damaged the person can no longer absorb the nutrients they need to thrive. They begin to have many symptoms, too numerous to list here.

There are over 300 symptoms of celiac disease. The most common are: bloating, diarrhea, constipation, fatigue, itchy skin rash, tingling or numbness, pale mouth sores, joint pain, delayed growth, poor weight gain, thin bones, infertility, headaches, depression, irritability and discolored teeth. There is also evidence to suggest that those who have been diagnosed with autism actually improve when given a gluten free diet. Information about celiac disease and its connection to autism can be found at www.celiaccentral.org

For persons with celiac disease the only way to get better at all is to stay completely away from gluten. They cannot eat anything with wheat, barley or rye in food or from a food manufacturer who does not isolate these grains from the processing of gluten free flours.

I was always a label reader. Now I have added reading the labels on packaging for foods that contain gluten.

The list of foods containing gluten is nearly endless. Fortunately because of the diagnosis of celiac disease many stores are stocking gluten-free products, but the cost is considerably more than wheat products.

It was at this point that I decided something had to be done. So after making bread for several months I began to work on recipes that I liked and started substituting the flours and experimenting with the combinations of ingredients. From this I have come up with recipes that really help those who need to be gluten free. The goodies are the things that most celiac patients miss the most. So that is why this book is so essential. They and anyone else can eat the tasty desserts and foods in this book.

We know that everyone's palate is different. Nothing will taste exactly the same to each person. That is why I made sure that these recipes were taste tested by those who do not have to be gluten-free as well as those who do. I hope you find the same thing that I did. I can be wheat and gluten-free and still enjoy many sweets like muffins, cakes and cookies once in a while without breaking the bank. In fact many of the recipes you find in this book actually taste better gluten-free.

One word of caution, don't taste the un-cooked dough! Something happens in the baking process that changes the taste. Also, many baked goods like muffins taste better after frozen and re-heated.

Now go out there and enjoy some gluten-free baking!

For further information you can go to my website at www.LindysLessons.com.

Sincerely,

Lindy Stein

Table of Contents

Helpful Hints 11

Desserts 13
    Pumpkin Cake 15
    Classic Fudge Brownies. 16
    Frosted Soft Sugar Cookies 17
    Chocolate Pecan Pie 18
    Pat-In-Pan Pie Crust 18
    Cream Cheese Apple Torte 19
    Banana Cake with Caramel Frosting 20
    Cherry-Vanilla Chip Cookies. 21
    Swirled Cheesecake 22
    Chocolate-Pecan Glazed Brownies 23
    Peanut Butter Brownie Cups 24
    Mount Pilot Cookies. 25
    Real Chocolate Chip Cookies. 26
    Chocolate-Peanut Butter Bars 27
    Peppermint Patty Cake 28
    Gingerbread 29
    "Have Mercy On My Soul" Chocolate Cookies 30
    Zucchini Carrot Cake. 31
    Chocolate-Pecan Torte 33
    Fudge-Nut Toffee Bars. 34
    Fudgy Zucchini Cake 35
    Snowy Chocolate Cookies. 36
    Peanut Butter Fudge Cups 37
    Fruit-Filled Crumb Cake 38
    Fudgy-Walnut Pie 39
    Frosted Fudge Brownies 40
    Pumpkin Chip Cookies. 41
    Mississippi Mud Brownies. 42
    Biscuit, Berries 'n Cream. 43
    German Chocolate Cake 45

Nutty Fudge Bars....46
Fudge Pudding Cake....47
Rich & Chocolaty Zucchini Brownies....48
Dotted Shortbread Cookies....49
Raspberry-Lover's Chocolate Cake....51
Rocky Road Brownies....52
Pecan-Caramel Cheesecake Pie....53
Peanut-Butter Cookie Pizza....54
Mock "Apple" Bars....55
Luscious Layered Brownies....56

Breads & Muffins....57
Pumpkin Cranberry Bread....58
Cherry Chip Muffins....59
Zucchini Bread with Brown Sugar Glaze....61
Coconut Biscuits....62
Chive 'n Cheddar Potato Muffins....63
Pumpkin Muffins with Chocolate Chips....64
Sweet Potato Biscuits....64
Cherry Pecan Bread....65
Apple-Praline Bread....66
Chocolate Chip Muffins....67
Peach Muffins....68
Squash Muffins....68
Chocolate Banana-Nut Bread....69
Dill Drop Biscuits....70
Corn Bread....70
Apple Streusel Muffins....71
Cream Cheese Filled Carrot Muffins....72
Secret Chocolate Muffins....73
Spiced Blueberry Muffins....74
Pumpkin Ginger Scones....75
Raspberry Chip Muffins....76

Breakfast....77
Berries 'n Cream Coffee Cake....78
Vanilla French Toast....79
Gingerbread Pancakes....80
Pineapple Coffee Cake....81
Pecan Pancakes....82

Chocolate Chip Coffee Cake. 83
Baked Maple French Toast 84
Nutmeg Coffee Cake 85
Coconut-Walnut Coffee Cake. 86
Pumpkin Pancakes. 87
Chocolate Cinnamon Coffee Cake 88
Strawberry Topped-Cream Cheese Filled-French Toast 89
Apple Pecan Pancakes 90
Chocolate Chip Pancakes. 90
Toffee-Topped Coffee Cake 91
Blueberry Brunch Casserole 92
Walnut-Cranberry Baked French Toast 93
Strawberry-Pecan Coffee Cake 94

Entrees 95
Creamed Chicken over Rice. 96
Nut-Crusted Baked Fish 97
Saucy Chicken 98
Baked Almond Chicken 99
Baked Cavatini. 100
Oven Baked Chicken Parmesan 101
Lots of Beef. 102
Baked Parmesan Fish 102
Crispy Herbed Coating 103
BBQ Meatballs 104
Meatballs and Sauce 105
Thick Beef Stew 106
Mini Cheddar Meat Loaves 107
Barbecued Chicken 'n Rice 108

Soups & Sandwiches 109
Chicken Pita Sandwiches 110
Parmesan Corn Chowder. 111
Fruit & Turkey Panini. 112
Delightful Chicken Pitas 113
Best Potato Soup 113
Italian Vegetable Soup. 114
Bountiful Harvest Pizza. 115
Toasted Cheese and Turkey 116

Glossary 117

Order a Copy of This Book. 119

Helpful Hints

Here is a list of main ingredients that I used often in this book:

Bob's Red Mill Gluten-Free All-Purpose Baking Flour
Xanthan Gum
Powdered Buttermilk
Aluminum-free baking powder

Helpful tips on baking with the recipes in this book

Bob's Red Mill Gluten-Free Baking Flour: Can be found in most grocery stores in the gluten-free area of the Healthy/Organic Foods section. Several stores also add the gluten-free products with regular products, ie: gluten free cake mixes can be found in the regular baking isle with regular cake mixes. This flour is referred to as *GF all-purpose flour* in this book.

GF: Stands for gluten-free. You will find that several of these recipes are naturally gluten-free.

Xanthan Gum: This can be purchased wherever gluten-free flours and baking items are sold.

Quantity of Xanthan Gum: These quantities are suggested for each cup of flour used. For example, if you are making cookies and the recipe calls for 2 cups of flour, you would use ½ teaspoon of xanthan gum.

¼ teaspoon for cookies
½ teaspoon for cakes
¾ teaspoon for muffins and quick breads
1–1 ½ teaspoon for yeast breads
2 teaspoons for pizza crust

Xanthan Gum must be added to the dry ingredients *before* liquid or wet ingredients are added.

Freezing Baked Items: If you are not able to use up a baked item within 2–3 days, it is best if it is frozen, then thawed and consumed. The dough will tend to get "doughy" or sticky as it ages. Most of the baked items in this book freeze very well.

Baking Pans: Stone, silicone, and stainless steel work best. I tried aluminum bake ware, but found that sometimes there was a metallic aftertaste.

Buttermilk: When a recipe calls for buttermilk, I substitute powdered buttermilk for regular buttermilk. This product must be stored in the refrigerator once it is opened. On the back of the powdered buttermilk can there is a chart explaining how to use it. Follow this chart. This will save you money and there will be no waste. Powdered buttermilk can be found in the baking isle of most grocery stores near the canned milk.

Chopped Nuts: When a recipe calls for "chopped nuts," chop them first, and then measure them. If it calls for "nuts, chopped," do the opposite—measure first, then chop.

Honey or Molasses: When measuring honey or molasses, spray or coat the inside of the measuring spoon or utensil with oil. The honey or molasses will slide right out.

Batter: If you are one who likes to dip your finger in the "cookie dough" - I strongly suggest that you refrain from doing so when using Bob's Red Mill Gluten-free All Purpose Baking Flour. Due to the natural bitterness of this flour, you may want to throw out the entire batch of dough before baking it!

French Toast: The bread used for the French Toast recipes comes from Bette Hagman's book, *The Gluten-Free Gourmet Bakes Bread*. Bette's *Four Flour Bread*, the cinnamon-nut variation.

Pita Bread: All pita bread referenced comes from Bette Hagman's book, *The Gluten-Free Gourmet Bakes Bread*.

Sandwich Bread: The bread used for the sandwiches comes from Bette Hagman's book, *The Gluten-Free Gourmet Bakes Bread*, the "Walnut Bread." However, I substitute sunflower seeds and canola oil for the walnuts and walnut oil. I also use Bob's Red Mill GF All-purpose Baking Flour instead of the flour it calls for.

Raw Sugar: If you prefer to use raw sugar the proportions are the same. However, be aware that because it is not refined you may have a grainy texture. Also, the moisture content is higher and therefore some recipes may be a little more moist.

GF Dry Bread Crumbs: GF bread crumbs may be purchased where gluten-free products are sold, or they can be easily made in your own kitchen. To make bread crumbs: save thinly sliced end pieces of GF bread in a zip lock freezer bag in your freezer. When desired amount of bread pieces is achieved, place bread on baking sheet or directly on oven rack. Heat oven to 200°F and dry bread out for 1–2 hours. Periodically check bread by trying to break it easily. Once bread is thoroughly dried out, cool completely. Process in a food processor until bread becomes fine crumbs. Store crumbs in a freezer safe container in the freezer.

Protein: Due to the high protein content of Bob's Red Mill Gluten-Free All-Purpose Baking Flour, the baked items will be more filling than those made with traditional wheat all-purpose flour.

Flavor: Some gluten-free items are better right from the oven and others are better after they have cooled. (Chocolate items need to "age" for best flavor.)

Baked Good Removal Tip: For easy removal from pans for bars or brownies, line pan with parchment paper or foil. Grease lining before adding batter.

13 desserts

"Life is uncertain, eat dessert first."
-Ernestine Ulmer

Gluten-Free Desserts

"I loved the fact that it was so moist! Heavenly!"
-Erica Beachy

"It looks and tastes GREAT! Really delicious!"
-Loretta Wagler

Pumpkin Cake

2 cups cooked pumpkin
4 eggs
1 cup vegetable oil
2 cups granulated sugar
2 cups GF all-purpose flour
1 teaspoon xanthan gum
1 teaspoon baking soda
1 teaspoon baking powder
1 teaspoon ground cinnamon, heaping
1 teaspoon salt
½ teaspoon pumpkin pie spice

FROSTING:
½ cup (1 stick) butter, softened
1 package (8 ounces) cream cheese*, softened
3 ½–4 cups powdered sugar

Preheat oven to 350°. Grease a 13-in. x 9-in. x 2-in. baking pan.

In a large mixing bowl, beat together the pumpkin, eggs and oil until well mixed.

In a separate bowl, whisk together the next eight ingredients. Gradually add to pumpkin mixture; mix well.

Pour batter into prepared baking pan and bake for 45–50 minutes or until toothpick inserted near the center comes out clean.

Cool completely on wire rack.

For frosting: in small mixing bowl, cream together butter and cream cheese. Gradually add powdered sugar until desired frosting consistency and sweetness is achieved.

Yield: 18 servings

"Excellent taste and texture – 4 of us tried it!"
—Alma Hurst

Classic Fudge Brownies

¾ cup 60% bittersweet chocolate chips
½ cup (1 stick) unsalted butter, cut into pieces
1 cup firmly packed brown sugar
1 teaspoon vanilla extract
2 eggs
¾ cup plus 2 tablespoons GF all-purpose flour
½ teaspoon salt
⅜ teaspoon xanthan gum
¼ teaspoon baking powder
½ cup semi-sweet chocolate chips

Preheat oven to 350°. Grease an 8-in. square baking pan.

In the top of a double boiler over barely simmering water, melt the chocolate and butter, stirring occasionally until smooth. Remove the pan from heat and let cool to room temperature.

Stir the brown sugar and vanilla into the chocolate mixture. Add the eggs and mix well.

In a bowl, whisk together the next four ingredients. Slowly fold the flour mixture into the chocolate mixture, mixing well until blended. Stir in the remaining chocolate chips and pour the batter into the prepared baking pan.

Bake for 30–35 minutes, or until a toothpick inserted near the center comes out clean. Remove from the oven and cool for at least 10 minutes before cutting into bars.

Yield: 16 brownies

"I liked everything about these. These brownies are the bomb! Very moist, melts in your mouth. Very chocolaty, yet not too sweet!"

-Nancy Florence

Frosted Soft Sugar Cookies

desserts

1 cup (2 sticks) butter (no substitutes), softened
¾ cup granulated sugar
2 eggs
1 teaspoon vanilla extract
½ teaspoon almond extract
2 cups GF all-purpose flour
1 teaspoon cream of tartar
½ teaspoon xanthan gum
½ teaspoon baking soda
¼ teaspoon ground nutmeg

FROSTING:
3 cups powdered sugar
¼ cup (½ stick) butter (no substitutes), softened
1 teaspoon almond extract
2–4 tablespoons hot water
Food coloring and sprinkles, optional

Preheat oven to 350°. Line cookie sheets with parchment paper.

In a large mixing bowl, cream butter and sugar. Beat in eggs, vanilla and almond extract.

In a separate bowl, whisk together next 5 ingredients. Gradually add to creamed mixture.

Drop by rounded teaspoonfuls 2 inches apart onto prepared cookie sheets.

Bake for 8–10 minutes or until light golden brown. Remove to wire rack to cool.

For frosting: in a medium bowl, combine powdered sugar, butter, almond extract and enough water to achieve nice spreading consistency. Tint with food coloring if desired.

Frost and sprinkle cookies.

Yield: 3 ½ dozen

*Note: These cookies are very soft and will fall apart easily.

"We liked the taste, frosting and sprinkles. Best sugar cookies *ever!*"
-Michael Dutt Family

"We liked the fact that these did not have overpowering sweetness."
-Teresa and Keli Geers

Pat-In-Pan Pie Crust

1 ½ cups plus 3 tablespoons GF all-purpose flour
1 tablespoon granulated sugar
¾ teaspoon xanthan gum
½ teaspoon salt
½ cup vegetable oil
3 tablespoons milk***

Place flour, sugar, xanthan gum and salt in pie pan and mix with your fingers until blended. In a measuring cup, combine oil and milk; beat with a fork until creamy. Pour oil and milk mixture over flour mixture and mix with a fork until completely moistened. Pat dough with your fingers up the sides of the pan first and then cover the bottom. Flute edges and fill.

*Note: for pre-baked crusts, prick bottom of crust with fork and bake for 25 minutes at 425°, checking often and pricking more if needed.

**Variation for 10-inch pie shells; 2 cups GF all-purpose flour, 1 tablespoon plus 1 teaspoon sugar, 1 teaspoon salt, ⅔ cup oil and 3 tablespoons milk.

Chocolate variety:

1 ½ cups plus 3 tablespoons GF all-purpose flour
¼ cup plus 1 tablespoon granulated sugar
¼ cup cocoa
¾ teaspoon xanthan gum
½ teaspoon salt
½ cup vegetable oil
3 tablespoons milk***

Place first 5 ingredients in pie pan and continue with same directions as above.

***Recipes were tested using fat free milk.

Chocolate Pecan Pie

4 squares (1 ounce each) semi-sweet baking chocolate
2 tablespoons unsalted butter
3 large eggs
1 cup light corn syrup
½ cup firmly packed brown sugar
1 teaspoon vanilla extract
⅛ teaspoon salt
1 ½ cups pecan halves*
1 Pat-in-pan pie crust, unbaked, using a 9-in. pie pan

Preheat oven to 325°. Prepare pat-in-pan crust.
In the top of a double boiler or in a heatproof bowl over barely simmering water, melt the chocolate and butter, stirring occasionally until smooth.

In a large bowl, beat eggs, corn syrup, brown sugar, vanilla and salt until blended. Beat in the chocolate mixture. Stir in the pecans and pour into prepared crust.

Bake for 55 minutes or until the filling is set**.

Cool completely on a wire rack.

Yield: 8 servings

*Feel free to substitute chopped pecans for pecan halves—the pie will be easier to cut when using pecan pieces.

**Allow longer baking time when using stone baking ware.

"It's good enough for 3rd's!"
-Chuck White

"Excellent taste. Texture of crust is excellent. Not too sweet, not too overwhelming."
-Nancy Florence

Cream Cheese Apple Torte

¾ cup (1 ½ sticks) butter, softened
½ cup granulated sugar
1 ½ cups GF all-purpose flour
¾ teaspoon xanthan gum
½ teaspoon pure vanilla extract

FILLING:
2 (8 ounces) packages cream cheese*, softened
¼ cup granulated sugar
2 eggs
¾ teaspoon pure vanilla extract

TOPPING:
3 cups thinly sliced peeled tart apples
½ cup granulated sugar
1 ¼ teaspoon ground cinnamon
½ teaspoon ground nutmeg

Preheat oven to 350°.

In a large bowl, combine first five ingredients. Press into the bottom of an ungreased 9-in. springform pan.

In a large mixing bowl, beat cream cheese and sugar until smooth. Add eggs and vanilla, mix well. Pour over crust.

Rinse out bowl used for filling and use for combining topping ingredients. When combined, spoon topping over filling.

Bake for 55—65 minutes or until the center is set.

Cool on wire rack.

Refrigerate until ready to serve.

Cut into wedges with serrated knife.

Note: Even a tight fitting springform pan may leak. To prevent drips, place a baking sheet on the rack underneath pan to catch the drips.

*Recipe was tested using one package of light cream cheese and one package of regular cream cheese.

"Excellent taste and texture! I loved the cream cheese and caramelized apple slices."
-Shashank Modak

Banana Cake with Caramel Frosting

½ cup shortening*
¾ cup packed brown sugar
½ cup granulated sugar
2 eggs
1 cup mashed ripe bananas (2–3 medium)
1 teaspoon vanilla extract
2 cups GF all-purpose flour
1 teaspoon baking soda
1 teaspoon xanthan gum
1 teaspoon salt
½ cup buttermilk**
½ cup chopped nuts

FROSTING:
½ cup packed brown sugar
¼ cup (½ stick) butter
6 tablespoons milk***
2 ½ to 3 cups powdered sugar

Preheat oven to 350°. Grease a 13-in. x 9-in. x 2-in. baking pan.

In a mixing bowl, cream the shortening and sugars. Add eggs, one at a time, beating well after each addition. Beat in bananas and vanilla.

In a separate bowl, whisk together the next four ingredients. Add to the creamed mixture alternately with buttermilk. Stir in nuts. Pour into prepared baking pan.

Bake for 25–30 minutes or until a toothpick inserted near the center comes out clean. Cool on a wire rack.

FROSTING:
Combine the brown sugar, butter and milk in a saucepan. Bring to a boil over medium heat; boil and stir for 2 minutes. Remove from the heat; cool to lukewarm.

Pour butter mixture into small mixing bowl. Gradually beat in powdered sugar until frosting reaches spreading consistency. Frost cooled cake.

Yield: 12 servings
*This recipe was tested using organic shortening.
**See Helpful Hints
***This recipe was tested with fat free milk.

"Very moist! The frosting was not too sweet. Delicious with hot tea!"
-Susan Pero

"The cake was very rich, make sure you have a glass of milk!"
-Alyssa Smith

Cherry-Vanilla Chip Cookies

1 cup (2 sticks) butter, softened
¾ cup granulated sugar
¾ cup packed brown sugar
2 eggs
¼ teaspoon almond extract
2 ⅔ cups GF all-purpose flour
1 teaspoon baking soda
⅝ teaspoon xanthan gum
½ teaspoon salt
1 package (10–12 ounces) vanilla or white chips
1 jar (10 ounces) maraschino cherries, drained and chopped

Preheat oven to 350°.

Line baking sheets with parchment paper.

In a large mixing bowl, cream butter and sugars. Add eggs, one at a time, beating well after each addition. Beat in almond extract.

In a separate bowl, whisk together the next four ingredients and gradually add to the creamed mixture. Stir in chips and cherries.

Drop by rounded tablespoonfuls 2 inches apart onto paper-lined baking sheets.

Bake for 9–11 minutes or until lightly browned. Remove paper from baking sheet to wire rack. Cool for 3–5 minutes.

Remove cookies from paper to wire rack. The parchment paper may be reused for next batch of dough.

Yield: 5 dozen

Swirled Cheesecake

4 squares (1 ounce each) semi-sweet baking chocolate
2 packages (8 ounces) cream cheese*, softened and *divided*
½ cup granulated sugar, *divided*
2 eggs, *divided*
½ teaspoon vanilla extract
1 Pat-in-pan pie crust, unbaked, using a 9-in. pie pan, chocolate variety (see page 18)

Prepare pie crust. Preheat oven to 350°.

Microwave chocolate in large microwavable bowl on high for 1–1 ½ minutes, stirring every 30 seconds. Stir until chocolate is completely melted.**

Add 1 package cream cheese, ¼ cup sugar and 1 egg to melted chocolate. Beat with a whisk until well blended. Pour into crust.

Using same bowl, whisk remaining cream cheese, sugar, egg and vanilla until well blended.

Spoon over batter; swirl gently with knife. Bake 40 minutes or until center is almost set. Cool. Refrigerate 3 hours or overnight. Let stand at room temperature 10 minutes before serving. Store any leftovers in refrigerator.

Yield: 8 servings

*Recipe was tested using one package of regular cream cheese and one package of light cream cheese.

**Do not heat the chocolate until it is completely melted, stir to melt remaining pieces.

> "Rich taste and cookie-like crust. I would never guess that I was eating a gluten-free cheesecake! I am excited to see and try more gluten-free recipes."
>
> -Nikki Neth

Chocolate-Pecan Glazed Brownies

½ cup (1 stick) butter, softened
1 cup granulated sugar
1 egg
¼ cup sour cream*
1 cup GF all-purpose flour
½ cup baking cocoa
½ teaspoon xanthan gum
½ teaspoon baking powder
¼ teaspoon salt
½ cup milk**

GLAZE:
¼ cup (½ stick) butter, softened
½ cup powdered sugar
2 tablespoons baking cocoa
3 tablespoons milk**
½ cup chopped pecans
½ teaspoon vanilla extract

Preheat oven to 350°. Grease a 13-in. x 9-in. x 2-in. baking pan.

In a large mixing bowl, cream butter and sugar. Beat in egg and sour cream.

In a separate bowl, whisk together the next 5 ingredients. Add to creamed mixture alternately with milk. Spread into prepared baking pan.

Bake for 20–25 minutes or until a toothpick inserted near the center comes out clean.

While brownie is baking prepare glaze. In small mixing bowl cream butter; gradually beat in powdered sugar, cocoa and milk. Stir in pecans and vanilla.

Spread over warm brownies. Cool on a wire rack.

Yield: 2 dozen

*This recipe was tested using light sour cream
**This recipe was tested using fat free milk

"Flavor and texture tasted like a regular brownie. Had I not known this was gluten-free, I would have never guessed it was not a "real" brownie!"
-Nikki Blank

Peanut Butter Brownie Cups

¾ cup granulated sugar
¼ cup (½ stick) butter, softened
1 tablespoon water
2 ¼ cups semi-sweet chocolate chips, *divided*
1 large egg
½ teaspoon vanilla extract
1 cup GF all-purpose flour
½ teaspoon xanthan gum
¼ teaspoon baking soda
¾ cup creamy peanut butter*

*Recipe was tested using Smart Balance™ Creamy Peanut Butter

Preheat oven to 350°. Grease a 12-cup muffin pan.

Place sugar, butter and water in a microwave safe bowl. Microwave on high power for 1 minute or until butter is melted, checking every 30 seconds. Add ¾ cup chocolate chips; stir until melted. Add egg and vanilla extract and stir well.

In a separate bowl, whisk together next three ingredients. Stir into chocolate mixture until blended. Allow to cool to room temperature. When chocolate mixture is cooled, stir in 1 cup chocolate chips. Spoon a heaping tablespoon of batter into each prepared muffin cup. Bake for 13–15 minutes or until top is set and a wooden pick inserted in center comes out still slightly wet. Place muffin pan on wire rack. Using the handle end of a wooden spoon, gently tap a hole in center of each brownie.

Place peanut butter in small, microwave safe bowl. Microwave on high power for 30 seconds; stir. If needed microwave for an additional 30 seconds. While brownies are still hot, spoon a scant tablespoon of peanut butter into center of each brownie. Top with remaining chocolate chips. Cool completely. Run a knife around edge of each brownie and carefully remove from pan.

Yield: 12 brownie cups

"Tasted great. I never would have guessed that the dessert was gluten-free!"
-Paula Ferguson

"One of the bestest desserts ever!"
-Nick Verbitsky, age 6

Mount Pilot Cookies

½ cup (1 stick) butter, softened
1 cup granulated sugar
1 egg
¼ cup milk*
1 teaspoon vanilla extract
1 ¾ cups GF all-purpose flour
⅓ cup baking cocoa, heaping
½ teaspoon salt
½ teaspoon baking soda
Scant ½ teaspoon xanthan gum
16–18 large marshmallows

ICING:
6 tablespoons butter (¾ stick), softened
2 tablespoons baking cocoa, heaping
¼ cup milk*
1 ¾ cups powdered sugar
½ teaspoon vanilla extract
Pecan halves

Preheat oven to 350°.

Line baking sheets with parchment paper. In a large mixing bowl, cream butter and sugar. Add egg, milk and vanilla; mix well.

In a separate bowl, whisk together the next five ingredients; beat into creamed mixture.

Drop by rounded teaspoonfuls onto prepared baking sheets. Bake for 8–8 ½ minutes.

Meanwhile, cut marshmallows in half. Place a marshmallow half, cut side down, onto each cookie.

Return to the oven for 2 minutes. Cool completely on wire rack.

For icing, in a small saucepan, combine butter, cocoa and milk. Bring to a boil; boil for 1 minute, stirring constantly.

Cool slightly; transfer to a small mixing bowl. Beat in powdered sugar and vanilla until smooth.

Spread over the cooled cookies. Top each with a pecan half.

Yield: about 3 dozen

*Recipe was tested using fat free milk

"The combination of chocolate, marshmallow and pecans with the chocolate sauce was wonderful and evenly balanced. A very tasty cookie that not only tasted good but was pleasing to the eye."
–Natasha Bruns

Real Chocolate Chip Cookies

2 ¾ cups GF all-purpose flour
1 teaspoon baking soda
1 teaspoon salt
⅝ teaspoon xanthan gum
1 cup (2 sticks) butter, softened
¾ cup granulated sugar
¾ cup packed brown sugar
2 large eggs
1 teaspoon vanilla extract
2 cups (12 ounces) semi-sweet chocolate chips*
1 cup chopped nuts (optional)

Preheat oven to 375°. Line baking sheets with parchment paper.

In a medium bowl, whisk together first four ingredients.

In a large mixing bowl, cream together butter and sugars. Add eggs, one at a time, beating well after each addition. Beat in vanilla.

Gradually beat in flour mixture. Stir in chocolate chips (and nuts).

Drop by rounded tablespoon onto prepared baking sheet. Bake for 9–11 minutes or until golden brown.

Cool on baking sheets for 2 minutes then remove to wire racks to cool completely.

Yield: about 5 dozen

*Optional: add 1 cup semi-sweet chocolate chips and 1 cup M&M® type candies.

> "Could not tell an alternate flour was used; tasted just like Toll House cookies."
> —Vicki Dutt

Chocolate-Peanut Butter Bars

¾ cup (1 ½ stick) butter, softened
1 ½ cups granulated sugar
3 eggs
1 teaspoon vanilla extract
1 ⅓ cups GF all-purpose flour
4 tablespoons baking cocoa
¾ teaspoon xanthan gum
½ teaspoon baking powder
½ teaspoon salt
½ cup chopped nuts, optional
4 cups miniature marshmallows

TOPPING:
1 ⅓ cups semi-sweet chocolate chips
1 cup peanut butter*
3 tablespoons butter
2 cups GF crisp rice cereal

Preheat oven to 350°. Line a 15-in. x 10-in. x 1-in. baking pan with foil. Grease foil-lined pan.

In a medium bowl, cream butter and sugar until light and fluffy. Add eggs, one at a time, beating well after each addition. Beat in vanilla.

In a separate bowl, whisk together the next five ingredients; gradually add to creamed mixture. Stir in nuts if desired. Spread in prepared baking pan. Bake for 15–18 minutes. Sprinkle with marshmallows; bake 2–3 minutes longer. Remove to a wire rack.

Cool completely.

For topping, combine the chocolate chips, peanut butter and butter in a small saucepan. Cook and stir over low heat until blended. Remove from the heat; stir in cereal. Spread over bars immediately. Chill.

Yield: about 3 dozen

*Recipe was tested using Smart Balance™ Creamy Peanut Butter

Note: to cut clean bars, run warm water over sharp knife, cut bars with wet knife. Clean knife after each cut.

"I liked the combination of flavors, no flavor overpowered the other. Just the right amount of chewiness."
-Teresa Geers

Peppermint Patty Cake

2 cups GF all-purpose flour
2 cups granulated sugar
1 teaspoon xanthan gum
1 teaspoon baking soda
1 cup (2 sticks) butter, softened
1 cup water
¼ cup (heaping) cocoa
½ cup buttermilk*
2 eggs, beaten
1 teaspoon vanilla extract

PEPPERMINT CREAM LAYER:
¾ cup (1 ½ stick) butter, softened
3 cups powdered sugar
milk**
1 teaspoon peppermint extract

CHOCOLATE GLAZE:
½ cup (1 stick) butter
1 cup semi-sweet chocolate chips
1 teaspoon vanilla extract

Preheat oven to 375°. Lightly grease 10-in.x15-in.x1-in. jelly roll pan.

In a large mixing bowl, whisk together first four ingredients. Combine butter, water and cocoa in a small saucepan; bring to a boil, stirring frequently.

Pour cocoa mixture over dry ingredients and mix well. Beat in buttermilk, eggs and vanilla until smooth. Pour into prepared pan. Bake 15–20 minutes or until cake tester comes out clean when inserted into center of cake.

Cool completely on wire rack. While cake is cooling mix butter, powdered sugar and enough milk to create an easily spreadable consistency. Add peppermint extract and combine well. Spread peppermint cream evenly over cooled cake and chill until set.

For chocolate glaze, place butter and chocolate chips in microwavable bowl. Microwave for 30 seconds, stir. Continue this pattern until all chocolate chips are melted. Stir in vanilla extract. Carefully pour chocolate glaze on top of cream layer. Cool. Cut into squares. Refrigerate leftovers.

Yield: about 4 dozen

*See Helpful Hints
**Recipe was tested using fat free milk

"I liked the delicious mint and chocolate flavor! Yum! This made a great birthday treat! It was not too rich. Thank you!"

-Joe Eckstein

Gingerbread

2 ¼ cups GF all-purpose flour
¼ cup granulated sugar
1 ½ teaspoon ground ginger
1 ⅛ teaspoon xanthan gum
1 teaspoon baking soda
1 teaspoon ground cinnamon
½ teaspoon salt
¼ teaspoon ground cloves
¼ ground nutmeg
½ cup (1 stick) butter, melted
¾ cup molasses
¼ cup water
1 egg
1 cup buttermilk*
½ cup diced crystallized ginger (optional)

Preheat oven to 350°. Grease and flour a 9-in. square pan.

In a large mixing bowl, whisk together the first nine ingredients.

Melt the butter in a microwave safe bowl. Add the molasses to the butter and pour into the dry ingredients, mixing to moisten. Add the water, stirring until everything is moistened.

Whisk together the egg and buttermilk. Stir into the batter until it is evenly combined. Stir in the crystallized ginger.

Pour the batter into the prepared pan, and bake for 30–35 minutes, until the cake just begins to pull away from the edge of the pan.

Remove from the oven and cool on wire rack for 15 minutes before slicing. Gingerbread is best served warm with whipped cream or ice cream.

Yield: 9 servings

*See Helpful Hints

"So moist and great gingerbread flavor. Best gingerbread I have ever eaten!"
-Ann Holden

"Very tasty, very moist!"
-Rhoda Hochstetler

"Have Mercy On My Soul" Chocolate Cookies

*Plan ahead, needs time to chill

2 cups 60% bittersweet chocolate chips
6 tablespoons (¾ stick) unsalted butter
3 large eggs
1 cup granulated sugar
⅓ cup GF all-purpose flour
½ teaspoon baking powder
Scant ⅛ teaspoon xanthan gum
2 cups semi-sweet chocolate chips
1 cup chopped walnuts

Melt the bittersweet chocolate chips and butter in the top of a double boiler or in a microwave safe bowl, stirring often until smooth. If using the microwave, stir every 30 seconds until chips are almost melted.

In a large mixing bowl, beat the eggs and sugar until thick; with a spoon stir in chocolate mixture. In a small bowl, whisk together the next 3 ingredients; stir into the chocolate mixture. Gently stir in the chocolate chips and nuts.

Using a sheet of plastic wrap, form the dough into two logs, each 2 inches in diameter and about 8 inches long. The dough will be quite soft. Wrap tightly and freeze for 30–45 minutes, or refrigerate for 1 hour or until firm.

Preheat oven to 375°. Line baking sheets with parchment paper. Unwrap the dough. With a sharp knife, cut the dough into ¾-inch slices. Place the slices 1 ½ inches apart on prepared baking sheets.

Bake for 12–14 minutes, until a shiny crust forms on top of the cookies but the interior is still soft. Let cookies cool on the cookie sheet. Store in airtight container at room temperature for up to one week.

Yield: 2 dozen cookies

"Fantastic! They are so excellent and rich!"
-Martha Shetler

"Amazingly good—brilliant—fabulously chocolaty!"
-Linder Shaw

Zucchini Carrot Cake

4 eggs
2 cups granulated sugar
1 ⅓ cups vegetable oil
2 ½ cups GF all-purpose flour
2 teaspoons baking soda
2 teaspoons baking powder
2 teaspoons ground cinnamon
1 ¼ teaspoons xanthan gum
1 teaspoon salt
1 teaspoon ground cloves
1 teaspoon ground ginger
½ teaspoon ground nutmeg
2 cups grated carrots
2 cups grated zucchini
1 cup coarsely chopped walnuts

FROSTING:
1 package (8 ounces) cream cheese, plus 1 package (3 ounces) cream cheese, softened
½ cup (1 stick), plus 3 tablespoons butter, softened
5 cups powdered sugar
2 teaspoons vanilla extract
Chopped walnuts for garnish, optional

Preheat oven to 350°. Grease three 9-in. round baking pans.

In a large mixing bowl, beat eggs and sugar until light and foamy. Gradually beat in oil.

In a separate mixing bowl, whisk together next nine ingredients; gradually add to batter. Beat for 4 minutes. Stir in carrots, zucchini and nuts. Pour into prepared baking pans. Bake for 35 minutes or until a toothpick inserted near the center comes out clean.

Cool for 5 minutes before removing from pans. Cool completely on wire racks.

FROSTING:
Beat cream cheese and butter in a large bowl until smooth. Add sugar and vanilla.

Continue to beat until sugar is dissolved.

Place one layer on serving plate, spread with frosting. Top with second layer and spread with frosting. Repeat with last layer; frost top and sides of cake.

Garnish with nuts if desired.

Yield: 12–14 servings

"Absolutely awesome! I really like it and so did my husband."
-Rose Eby

"Super! We ate this cake for my birthday cake!"
-Perry and Miriam Beachy

"The cake was moist and had good flavor."
-Mary Harig

"So smooth a taste, delightful! Great dessert, not so sweet—which is great for me."
-Grace Raber

Chocolate-Pecan Torte

4 large eggs, separated
½ cup granulated sugar
⅔ cup GF all-purpose flour
½ teaspoon baking soda
⅜ teaspoon xanthan gum
¼ teaspoon salt
¾ cup ground pecans
⅓ cup baking cocoa
¼ cup water
1 teaspoon vanilla extract
¼ cup sugar

CHOCOLATE FROSTING:
⅔ cup powdered sugar
⅓ cup baking cocoa
2 cups whipping cream
1 ½ teaspoons vanilla extract

¾ cup chopped pecans, toasted

RICH CHOCOLATE GLAZE:
2 tablespoons baking cocoa
2 tablespoons water
1 tablespoon butter or margarine
1 cup sifted powdered sugar
¼ teaspoon vanilla extract

Preheat oven to 375°. Grease bottoms of two (9-inch) round cake pans. Line bottom of pans with wax paper; grease wax paper. Set pans aside.

In large mixing bowl, beat egg yolks at high speed; gradually add ½ cup sugar; beating until mixture is thick and pale.

In a separate bowl, whisk together the next six ingredients; add to egg yolk mixture alternately with water; beginning and ending with flour mixture. Stir in vanilla.

In a small bowl, beat egg whites at high speed until foamy; gradually add ¼ cup sugar, beating until stiff peaks form. Fold into batter. Pour batter into prepared pans.

Bake for 16–18 minutes or until a toothpick inserted in center comes out clean.

Cool in pans on wire racks 10 minutes; remove from pans, and cool completely on wire racks.

While cake layers are cooling, prepare frosting. In a medium mixing bowl, combine sugar and cocoa; gradually stir in cream and vanilla. Beat at low speed until mixture is blended; then beat at high speed until stiff peaks form.

Split layers in half horizontally to make 4 layers*.

Place one layer on a serving plate; spread 1 cup Chocolate Frosting on top of layer. Repeat procedure with second and third layers and 2 additional cups frosting.

Top stack with fourth layer. Spread remaining frosting on sides of cake; press chopped pecans into frosting.

To prepare Rich Chocolate Glaze, in a small saucepan, combine first 3 ingredients; cook over medium heat, stirring constantly, until mixture thickens. Remove from heat; stir in sugar and vanilla.

Spread Rich Chocolate Glaze over top.

*To split cake layers: after the cake layers have cooled, insert toothpicks around the outside of each layer halfway up the side. Make sure toothpicks are at the same level and lined up evenly around the cake. Use a long serrated knife (a large bread knife works well), rest the blade flat on the toothpicks. Using the toothpicks as guides, carefully slice the cake horizontally, keeping the cake in place with your other hand. Remove toothpicks and carefully lift one layer to serving plate.

Yield: 12 servings

Fudge-Nut Toffee Bars

1 ¾ cups GF all-purpose flour
¾ cup powdered sugar
¼ cup baking cocoa
¾ teaspoon xanthan gum
¾ cup (1 ½ sticks) cold butter, no substitutes
1 can (14 ounces) sweetened condensed milk
2 cups (12 ounces) semi-sweet chocolate chips, *divided*
1 teaspoon vanilla extract
1 cup coarsely chopped walnuts
½ cup flaked coconut
½ cup English toffee bits or almond brickle chips

Preheat oven to 350°. Grease a 13-in. x 9-in. x 2-in. baking pan.

In a medium bowl, whisk together the first four ingredients. Cut in butter until mixture resembles coarse crumbs.

Press firmly into prepared baking pan. Bake for 10 minutes.

Meanwhile, in a microwave safe bowl, heat milk and 1 cup chocolate chips at 30 second intervals, stirring after each 30 seconds until chocolate chips are melted. Stir in vanilla.

Pour filling over crust. Sprinkle with the walnuts, coconut, toffee bits and remaining chocolate chips; press down firmly.

Bake for 18–20 minutes or until set. Cool on a wire rack.

Cut into bars.

Yield: 3 dozen

"Awesome texture! I liked the combination of brownie, toffee and coconut. Can I have more?"
-Jeff Berridge

Fudgy Zucchini Cake

½ cup (1 stick) butter, softened
1 ½ cups granulated sugar
3 eggs
½ cup vegetable oil
1 tablespoon vanilla extract
1 ¾ cups GF all-purpose flour
⅓ cup baking cocoa
2 teaspoons baking soda
1 teaspoon baking powder
⅞ teaspoon xanthan gum
½ teaspoon ground cinnamon
2 cups shredded zucchini
1 cup chopped walnuts, optional
¾ cup semi-sweet chocolate chips
¾ cup vanilla or white chips

Preheat oven to 350°.

Grease 13-in. x 9-in. x 2-in. baking pan.

In a large mixing bowl, cream butter and sugar.

Add eggs, one at a time, beating well after each addition.

Beat in oil and vanilla.

In a medium bowl, whisk together the next six ingredients; gradually add to creamed mixture.

Fold in zucchini and walnuts if desired.

Spread into prepared pan.

Sprinkle chips over batter* and bake for 30–35 minutes or until a toothpick inserted near the center comes out clean.

Cool on wire rack.

Yield: 12–15 servings

*Option: Let cake bake for 15 minutes, then sprinkle with chocolate and vanilla chips. Continue baking. The chips will not sink into the cake, but will become a topping instead.

"Very light and fluffy, liked the vanilla/chocolate chip combination!"
-Julie Grimm

"Wow, this is gluten free? Very yummy!"
-Nancy Ikels

Snowy Chocolate Cookies

*Plan ahead, needs time to chill

½ cup (1 stick) butter, softened
4 squares (1 ounce each) unsweetened baking chocolate
3 large eggs
2 cups granulated sugar
2 teaspoons baking powder
2 teaspoons vanilla extract
¼ teaspoon salt
2 cups GF all-purpose Flour
½ teaspoon xanthan gum
⅔ cup powdered sugar

In a sauce pan, melt butter and baking chocolate, stirring often. Set aside to cool.

In a medium bowl, combine next five ingredients. Add chocolate mixture; blending well. In a separate bowl, whisk together flour and xanthan gum; gradually add to chocolate mixture, stirring until thoroughly combined.

Cover and refrigerate for 2 hours.

After dough has chilled, preheat oven to 375°. Line baking sheets with parchment paper.

Pour powdered sugar into a shallow pan or bowl.

Shape dough into 1-inch balls and roll in powdered sugar, coating generously.

Place 2 inches apart on prepared baking sheet.

Bake 10–15 minutes or until set.

Cool on baking sheet 2 minutes.

Remove to wire rack and cool completely.

Yield: 3 dozen cookies

"Very moist cookie, great flavor."
-Jennifer Shugert

"I liked the powdered sugar on top and chewy middle, a lot! Very chocolaty!"
-Jessica Brown, 14 yrs old

Peanut Butter Fudge Cups

*Plan ahead, needs time to chill

½ cup (1 stick) butter, softened
½ cup creamy peanut butter*
½ cup granulated sugar
½ cup packed brown sugar
1 egg
½ teaspoon vanilla extract
1 ¼ cup GF all-purpose flour
¾ teaspoon baking soda
½ teaspoon salt
scant ⅜ teaspoon xanthan gum

FUDGE FILLING:
1 cup milk chocolate chips
1 cup semi-sweet chocolate chips
1 can (14 ounces) sweetened condensed milk
1 teaspoon vanilla extract
chopped peanuts (optional)

Lightly grease two 24-cup mini muffin pans.

In a large mixing bowl, cream the butter, peanut butter and sugars. Beat in egg and vanilla.

In a separate bowl, whisk together the next four ingredients. Gradually add to creamed mixture.

Chill for 1 hour.

Preheat oven to 325°. Shape into 48 balls, 1 in. each. Place in prepared mini-muffin pans.

Bake for 14–16 minutes or until lightly browned.

Using the end of a wooden spoon handle, make a ⅜ to ½ in. deep indentation in the center of each ball. Cool in pans for 5 minutes before removing to wire racks to cool completely.

For filling, melt chocolate chips in microwave or in sauce pan on stove top. Stir in milk and vanilla until smooth. Spoon filling into each shell. Sprinkle with peanuts.

(Leftover filling can be stored in the refrigerator and served warm over ice cream.)

Yield: 4 dozen

*Recipe was tested using Smart Balance™ Creamy Peanut Butter

"I love how moist the cookie is! I have celiac disease so I eat a lot of gluten-free baked goods, but these are one of the best cookies I have ever tasted!"

-Jordan Keiner

Fruit-Filled Crumb Cake

⅔ cup cup granulated sugar
¼ cup cornstarch
¾ cup water
2 cups fresh or frozen unsweetened raspberries, blueberries or strawberries
1 tablespoon lemon juice

CRUST:
3 cups GF all-purpose flour
1 cup granulated sugar
1 tablespoon baking powder
1 ½ teaspoon xanthan gum
1 teaspoon salt
1 teaspoon ground cinnamon
½ teaspoon ground nutmeg
1 cup cold butter, cubed
2 eggs
1 cup milk*
1 teaspoon vanilla extract

TOPPING:
½ cup GF all-purpose flour
½ cup granulated sugar
¼ teaspoon ground cinnamon
¼ cup cold butter
⅓ cup sliced almonds

Grease a 13-in. x 9-in. x 2-in. baking pan.

In a saucepan, combine sugar, cornstarch, fruit and water. Bring to a boil over medium heat; boil for 5 minutes or until thickened, stirring constantly. Remove from heat; stir in lemon juice. Cool.

Preheat oven to 350°.

While fruit mixture is cooling, whisk together first seven crust ingredients. Cut in butter until mixture resembles coarse crumbs.

In a small bowl, beat eggs, milk and vanilla; add to crumb mixture and mix well. Spread two-thirds of the mixture into prepared baking pan. Spoon fruit filling over crust to within 1 inch of the edges. Spoon remaining crust mixture over filling.

For topping, combine flour, sugar and cinnamon, cut in butter until crumbly. Stir in almonds and sprinkle over top of the cake.

Bake for 50–55 minutes or until lightly browned.

Yield: 20–24 servings

*Recipe was tested using fat free milk

"Not too sweet, I liked the raspberry filling and crumbly topping. I would not have known it was gluten free. Nice taste and texture."

–Ken Schloemer

Fudgy-Walnut Pie

1 Pat-in-pan pie crust (see page 18), unbaked, using a 9-in. pie pan
½ cup packed brown sugar
¼ cup GF all-purpose flour
3 eggs, lightly beaten
¼ cup (1/2 stick) butter, melted
1 teaspoon vanilla extract
2 cups semi-sweet chocolate chips, melted
1 cup walnuts, coursely chopped
Chocolate syrup, optional
Ice cream of choice

Prepare pie crust as directed for a 9-in. pie plate.

Preheat oven to 375°.

In a large mixing bowl combine sugar, flour, eggs, butter, vanilla, melted chips and nuts. Pour into pie crust.

Bake for 25–30 minutes or until set.

Cool on a wire rack.

Serve with chocolate syrup and ice cream if desired.

Yield: 8 servings

"Wonderful! I would buy a book just for this recipe!"
-Rachel Clark

Frosted Fudge Brownies

1 cup (2 sticks) butter (no substitutes), softened
2 cups granulated sugar
4 eggs
3 squares (1 ounce each) unsweetened baking chocolate, melted
2 teaspoons vanilla extract
1 ½ cups GF all-purpose flour
1 teaspoon baking powder
1 teaspoon salt
¾ teaspoon xanthan gum
1 cup chopped walnuts

FROSTING:
⅓ cup (5 ⅓ tablespoons) butter (no substitutes)
3 cups powdered sugar
1 ½ teaspoons vanilla extract
4–5 tablespoons whipping cream

TOPPING:
1 square (1 ounce) unsweetened baking chocolate
1 tablespoon butter (no substitute)
1 tablespoon powdered sugar

Preheat oven to 350°. Grease or foil line a 15-in. x 10-in. x 1-in. baking pan.

In a mixing bowl, cream butter and sugar. Add eggs, one at a time, beating well after each addition. Add chocolate and vanilla; mix well.

In a separate bowl, whisk together the next four ingredients; add to creamed mixture and mix well. Stir in walnuts.

Spread into prepared baking pan. Bake for 25–30 minutes or until a toothpick inserted near the center comes out clean.

Cool on a wire rack. For frosting, melt butter in microwave safe bowl. Pour into a mixing bowl; add powdered sugar, vanilla and enough cream to achieve spreading consistency. Frost cooled brownies.

For topping, melt chocolate and butter; stir until smooth. Add powdered sugar; stir until smooth. Drizzle over frosting. Cut into bars.

Yield: 4 dozen

"I liked the light texture. They were delicious!"
-Diane Strunkenberg

"We liked these very much! We ate one right away and all thought it was marvelous!"
-Mary Jane Yoder

Pumpkin Chip Cookies

1 cup (2 sticks) butter, softened
½ cup granulated sugar
½ cup packed brown sugar
1 egg
2 teaspoons pure vanilla extract
1 cup canned pumpkin
2 cups GF all-purpose flour
3 ½ teaspoons pumpkin pie spice
1 teaspoon baking powder
1 teaspoon baking soda
½ teaspoon xanthan gum
¼ teaspoon salt
1 package (11 ounces) vanilla or white chips

FROSTING: (optional)
½ cup packed brown sugar
3 tablespoons butter
¼ cup milk*
1 ½–2 cups powdered sugar

Preheat oven to 350°.

Line baking sheets with parchment paper.

In a large mixing bowl, cream butter and sugars until light and fluffy. Beat in next three ingredients until well combined.

In a separate mixing bowl, whisk together next six ingredients. Gradually add to the pumpkin mixture and mix well.

Stir in chips.

Drop by rounded teaspoonfuls 2 inches apart onto prepared baking sheets. Bake for 12–14 minutes or until firm.

Remove to wire racks to cool.

For frosting, combine brown sugar and butter in a small saucepan. Bring to a boil over medium heat; boil for one minute or until slightly thickened, stirring constantly.

Cool 10 minutes. Transfer to a small mixing bowl. Add milk and beat until smooth. Beat in enough powdered sugar to reach desire spreading consistency.

Spread over cooled cookies.

Yield: 5 dozen

"Excellent taste and texture! If I could make cookies this soft!!"
-Rhoda Hochstetler

"Very moist and yummy!"
-Jodie Keene

Mississippi Mud Brownies

4 (1-ounce each) squares unsweetened baking chocolate
1 cup (2 sticks) butter
2 cups granulated sugar
1 cup GF all-purpose flour
½ teaspoon xanthan gum
⅛ teaspoon salt
4 large eggs, lightly beaten
1 cup chopped pecans
2 (1-ounce each) squares unsweetened baking chocolate
½ cup evaporated milk
½ cup (1 stick) butter
½ teaspoon vanilla extract
4 ½–5 cups powdered sugar
3 cups miniature marshmallows

Preheat oven to 350°. Grease and flour a 13-in. x 9-in. x 2-in. baking pan. Combine 4 chocolate squares and 1 cup butter in a large saucepan; cook over low heat, stirring until chocolate and butter melt. Remove from heat.

Whisk together next four ingredients; add to melted chocolate mixture. Add eggs and pecans; stir until blended. Spoon batter into prepared pan. Bake for 30–35 minutes or until a wooden pick inserted in center comes out clean.

Meanwhile, combine 2 chocolate squares, milk and ½ cup butter in a heavy saucepan. Cook over low heat, stirring often, until chocolate and butter melt. Remove from heat. Transfer to a medium mixing bowl. Stir in vanilla. Gradually add powdered sugar, beating at low speed with an electric mixer until frosting is smooth.

Sprinkle marshmallows evenly over warm brownies. Quickly pour frosting over marshmallows, spreading evenly. Cool completely in pan on a wire rack. Cut into bars.

Yield: 2 dozen

* Note: to cut clean bars, run warm water over sharp knife, cut bars with wet knife. Clean knife after each cut.

"It feels like it is supposed to be in your mouth."
-Jonathan Holden age 16

"I could probably try a couple more samples to provide more definitive feedback!"
-Kevin Cline

Biscuit, Berries 'n Cream

4 cups sliced fresh strawberries
½ cup plus 1 tablespoon granulated sugar, *divided*
2 cups GF all-purpose flour
1 teaspoon xanthan gum
1 teaspoon baking powder
½ teaspoon salt
½ teaspoon baking soda
⅓ cup shortening
¾ cup buttermilk*
2 tablespoons butter, melted
1 teaspoon cinnamon
1 cup heavy whipping cream
¼ cup honey

Preheat oven to 400°. Line two baking sheets with parchment paper. In a small bowl, combine strawberries and ½ cup sugar; cover and refrigerate until serving.

In a large bowl, whisk together the next five ingredients. Cut in shortening until mixture resembles coarse crumbs. Stir in buttermilk until a soft dough forms.

Divide dough in half. On prepared baking sheets, gently pat each portion of dough into an 8-inch circle; brush with butter.

Mix together cinnamon and remaining sugar. Sprinkle on top of biscuits. Bake for 13–15 minutes or until golden brown.

Remove to wire racks to cool.

In a large bowl, beat cream until it begins to thicken. Add honey; beat until stiff peaks form.

Place one biscuit on a serving platter; layer with half of the strawberries and whipped cream. Top with remaining biscuit, berries and cream.

Serve immediately. Refrigerate leftovers.

Yield: 8 servings

*See Helpful Hints

"Very refreshing summer dessert. Not too sweet."
-Joe Eckstein

"Very smooth texture and moist. Taste was excellent. Jim said he'd have another piece when he got home!"
-Barb and Jim Lawrenz

German Chocolate Cake

"The cake was very moist and the icing was great. I would make this."
—Mary Harig

CAKE:
4 squares (1 ounce each) semi-sweet baking chocolate
½ cup water
1 cup (2 sticks) unsalted butter, softened
2 cups granulated sugar
4 large eggs, separated
1 teaspoon vanilla extract
2 cups GF all-purpose flour
1 teaspoon baking soda
1 teaspoon xanthan gum
1 cup buttermilk**
½ teaspoon salt

BUTTER PECAN FROSTING*:
½ cup (1 stick) butter
1 cup half-an-half
1 cup firmly packed light or dark brown sugar
3 large egg yolks
1 teaspoon vanilla extract
1 cup chopped pecans
1 cup flaked coconut

Preheat oven to 350°. Line three 8-inch or 9-inch cake pans with parchment paper.

In the top of a double boiler or in a heatproof bowl over barely simmering water, melt the chocolate with the ½ cup water, stirring until smooth.

In a large bowl, cream the butter with the sugar until light and fluffy. Add the egg yolks, one at a time, beating after each addition. Mix in the melted chocolate and vanilla.

In a separate bowl, whisk together the next three ingredients.

Add the dry ingredients alternately with the buttermilk to the chocolate mixture. Mix until smooth.

In a small bowl, beat the egg whites with the salt until very stiff peaks form. Fold into the batter.

Spread into prepared pans. Bake for 30–35 minutes or until toothpick inserted near the center comes out clean.

Cool on a wire rack for 10 minutes; remove the cakes from the pans. Cool completely and peel off the parchment paper before frosting.

To make the frosting, in a heavy sauce pan over medium heat, melt the butter completely. Add the half-and-half, brown sugar and egg yolks, blending with a whisk until the mixture begins to boil.

Reduce to low heat and continue to stir for 5–7 minutes, until the frosting has thickened. Add the vanilla, then fold in the pecans and coconut.

To assemble the cake, place one layer on serving plate, spread some of the frosting over the top of this layer. Place a second layer on top and frost. Repeat with the third layer.

*Make a double batch of frosting if you wish to frost the sides of the cake as well.
**See Helpful Hints

Yield: one 3-layer cake

Nutty Fudge Bars

1 cup butter (2 sticks), softened
2 cups GF all-purpose flour
½ cup granulated sugar
1 teaspoon xanthan gum
¼ teaspoon salt
1 can (14 ounce) sweetened condensed milk
2 cups (12 ounces) semi-sweet chocolate chips, *divided*
1 teaspoon vanilla extract
¾ cup chopped walnuts
¾ cup chopped pecans
½ cup milk chocolate chips

Preheat oven to 350°. Grease a 13-in. x 9-in. x 2-in. baking pan.

In a large bowl, beat butter until fluffy.

In a separate bowl, whisk together the next four ingredients; add to butter and beat until crumbly. Set aside 1 cup for topping. Press remaining crumb mixture into prepared baking pan.

Bake for 15–20 minutes or until set and edges begin to brown. While crust is baking, in a small saucepan or microwave safe bowl, combine milk and 1 ½ cups semi-sweet chocolate chips. Cook and stir until chips are melted. If using the microwave method—cook for 30 second intervals and stir until chips are melted. Stir in vanilla when chips are melted. Spread chocolate mixture over crust.

Combine nuts, milk chocolate chips, remaining semi-sweet chocolate chips and reserved crumb mixture. Sprinkle over chocolate layer. Bake for 15–20 minutes or until center is set. Cool on wire rack. Cut into bars.

Yield: 3 dozen

"Loved this! Good combination of chocolate with crust and nut topping."
-Leeann Gallaway

"I liked the rich chocolate taste and looks. They stayed fresh tasted for several days."
-Babs Graber

Fudge Pudding Cake

desserts

1 cup GF all-purpose flour
⅓ cup premium unsweetened cocoa*
2 teaspoons baking powder
½ teaspoon xanthan gum
¼ teaspoon salt
1 ¼ cups granulated sugar, *divided*
½ cup milk**, at room temperature
3 tablespoons vegetable oil
1 teaspoon vanilla extract
½ cup firmly packed brown sugar
⅓ cup (heaping) premium unsweetened cocoa
1 ½ cup boiling water
Whipped cream or ice cream

Preheat oven to 350°. Lightly grease an 8-in. square pan.

In large mixing bowl, whisk together first five ingredients and ¾ cup sugar in a large bowl; stir in milk, oil and vanilla.

Spread batter in prepared pan.

In a separate bowl, combine brown sugar, cocoa and remaining ½ cup granulated sugar; sprinkle over batter in pan.

Using a spoon, gently drizzle 1 ½ cups boiling water over batter, being careful not to disturb layers; it's the water that creates the pudding layer while the cake bakes. (Do not stir.)

Bake for 45 minutes or until a cake layer forms on top and layer springs back when touched.

Cool on a wire rack 25 minutes.

Serve warm with whipped cream or ice cream.

Yield: 6–8 servings

*For richer chocolate flavor use ½ cup unsweetened cocoa
**Recipe was tested using fat free milk

"This is good enough to serve in a fine restaurant!"
-Heather Manger

"It's like a chocolate massage for the mouth."
-Don Clark

Rich & Chocolaty Zucchini Brownies

1 ½ cups granulated sugar
½ cup vegetable oil
1 egg, slightly beaten
2 teaspoons vanilla extract
2 cups GF all-purpose flour
½ cup, rounded, baking cocoa
1 ½ teaspoons baking soda
1 teaspoon xanthan gum
¼ teaspoon salt
2 cups shredded zucchini
1 package (12 ounces) semi-sweet chocolate chips
½ cup chopped nuts, optional

Preheat oven to 325°. Grease a 9-in. x 13-in. x 2-in. baking pan

In a large mixing bowl, stir together sugar and oil; add egg and vanilla, stir well.

In a separate bowl, whisk together the next five ingredients; add to sugar and egg mixture; stir until moistened. Fold in zucchini, chocolate chips and nuts.

Spread in prepared pan.

Bake for 35–40 minutes or until toothpick inserted near center comes out clean.

Yield: 15–18 servings

"I liked the chunks of chocolate. My two friends were skeptical about trying this since it was gluten-free, but they *loved* it!"
-Brooke Slaughter

"Very rich and chocolaty!"
-Tracey Troyer

Dotted Shortbread Cookies

1 cup (2 sticks) butter (no substitutes), softened
½ cup granulated sugar
1 teaspoon vanilla extract
2 cups GF all-purpose flour
½ teaspoon xanthan gum
¼ cup corn starch
1 cup M&M® chocolate candies

Preheat oven to 300°. Line baking sheet with parchment paper.

In a large mixing bowl, cream butter, sugar and vanilla using electric mixer.

In another bowl, whisk together the next three ingredients. Gradually add flour mixture to butter mixture. Mix until well combined.

Shape dough into 1-inch balls and place on parchment lined baking sheets. Gently flatten each cookie using fingers or a flat bottomed drinking glass (dipped in sugar to prevent sticking).

Place 5–6 M&M® candies on top of each cookie.

Bake for 25–30 minutes, or until bottoms begin to brown.

Cool for 5 minutes, remove to a wire rack to cool completely.

Yield: 3 dozen

> "Very simple but good."
> -Teresa Geers

> "Reminded me of the M&M® ice cream sandwich. Good with milk."
> -Lizzie Pero, age 10

"The flavor was incredible! My taste buds literally sang a symphony from the exciting mixture of flavors!"
-Audretta Hall

Raspberry-Lover's Chocolate Cake

3 cups granulated sugar
2 ¾ cups GF all-purpose flour
1 cup baking cocoa
2 teaspoons baking soda
1 ½ teaspoons salt
1 ⅜ teaspoons xanthan gum
¾ teaspoon baking powder
1 ¼ cups buttermilk*
¾ cup canola oil
3 teaspoons vanilla extract
3 eggs
1 ½ cups (12 ounces) coca cola, room temperature

FILLING:
4 tablespoons seedless raspberry jam, melted
3 tablespoons GF all-purpose flour
6 tablespoons milk**
6 tablespoons shortening
3 tablespoons butter, softened
3 cups powdered sugar
2 tablespoons raspberry extract
¼ teaspoon salt

FROSTING:
1 package (8 ounces) cold cream cheese
⅓ cup butter, softened
½ cup baking cocoa
1 tablespoon raspberry extract
4 cups powdered sugar

Preheat oven to 350°. Grease three 9-in. round cake pans. Line with wax paper and grease paper; set aside. In a large mixing bowl, whisk together the first seven ingredients.

In a separate bowl, combine buttermilk, oil and vanilla; mix into dry ingredients. Add eggs, one at a time, beating well after each addition; beat for 2 minutes. Gradually add coca cola (batter will be thin). Pour batter into prepared pans. Bake for 35–40 minutes or until a toothpick inserted near the center comes out clean. Cool for 10 minutes before removing from pans to wire racks to cool completely; peel off waxed paper. Place one cake layer on a serving plate; spread with about 2 tablespoons jam. Place remaining layers on waxed paper; spread one of the remaining layers with remaining jam. Let stand for 30 minutes.

For filling, in a small saucepan, whisk together the flour and milk until smooth. Cook over medium heat for 1 minute or until thickened, stirring constantly. Remove from the heat and let stand until cool. In a large mixing bowl, cream shortening and butter. Gradually add powdered sugar; mix well. Gradually add cooled milk mixture; beat for 4 minutes or until light and fluffy. Beat in extract and salt.

Spread half of the filling over cake layer on the plate to within ¼ inch of the edge. Top with the other jam-covered cake layer, then spread with remaining filling. Top with remaining cake layer. In a large bowl, beat cream cheese and butter until smooth. Add cocoa and extract; mix well. Gradually add powdered sugar; beat until light and fluffy. Frost top and sides of cake. Store in refrigerator.

Yield: 16 servings

*See Helpful Hints
**Recipe was tested using fat free milk

NOTE: To enhance chocolate flavor in the cake layers, it is recommended to let the layers sit overnight (they can be put back into their pans, keeping the wax paper on each layer and cover pans with foil).

> "Great texture, very moist. This cake is one to die for, especially the raspberry filling! It looked very eloquent, great appearance."
> —Sue York

Rocky Road Brownies

¾ cup butter (1 ½ sticks)
4 squares (1 ounce each) unsweetened baking chocolate
4 eggs
2 cups granulated sugar
1 teaspoon vanilla extract
1 cup GF all-purpose flour
½ teaspoon xanthan gum
2 cups miniature marshmallows
1 cup (6 ounces) semi-sweet chocolate chips
½ cup chopped walnuts

Preheat oven to 350°. Grease a 13-in. x 9-in. x 2-in. baking pan.

In a saucepan over low heat, melt butter and chocolate; cool for 10 minutes.

In a mixing bowl, beat eggs, sugar and vanilla. Stir in chocolate mixture.

In a separate bowl, whisk together the flour and xanthan gum; add to chocolate mixture and mix well.

Spread in prepared pan.

Bake for 25–30 minutes or until a toothpick inserted near the center comes out clean.

Sprinkle with marshmallows, chocolate chips and walnuts; bake for 3–4 minutes longer or until marshmallows begin to puff.

Cool on a wire rack.

Yield: 2 dozen

"We need another plate of these to determine the texture!"
-Harry Conte

"We loved everything about these! Absolutely delicious!"
-Gowans Family

Pecan-Caramel Cheesecake Pie

1 Pat-in-pan pie crust, unbaked, using a 9-in. pie pan (see page 18)
1 package (8 ounces) cream cheese, softened
½ cup granulated sugar
4 eggs
1 teaspoon vanilla extract
1 ¼ cups chopped pecans
1 cup caramel ice cream topping

Prepare Pat-in-pan crust.

Preheat oven to 375°

In a small bowl, beat the cream cheese, sugar, 1 egg and vanilla until smooth. Spread into pie crust; sprinkle with pecans.

Rinse out small bowl. Use this bowl to whisk remaining eggs; gradually whisk in caramel topping until blended. Pour over pecans.

Bake for 40–45 minutes or until lightly browned and center is set (loosely cover with foil after 20 minutes if pie is browning too quickly).

Cool on wire rack.

Refrigerate for 4 hours or overnight before serving. Refrigerate leftovers.

Yield: 6–8 servings

"For a person who doesn't like cheesecake, this was amazing!"
-Hannah Bergman, age 13

Peanut-Butter Cookie Pizza

½ cup (1 stick) butter, softened
½ cup granulated sugar
½ cup packed brown sugar
½ cup creamy peanut butter*
1 egg
½ teaspoon vanilla extract
1 ½ cup GF all-purpose flour
⅜ teaspoon xanthan gum
2 cup miniature marshmallows
1 cup semi-sweet chocolate chips

Preheat oven to 375°. Grease a 15-in. pizza pan.

In large mixing bowl, cream together butter, sugars and peanut butter. Add egg and vanilla extract.

In a separate bowl, whisk together flour and xanthan gum, gradually add to creamed mixture.

Press dough evenly on prepared pizza pan.

Bake for 10–13 minutes.

Sprinkle with marshmallows and chocolate chips.

Bake 5–8 minutes longer or until marshmallows are lightly brown.

Yield: 10–12 servings

*Recipe was tested using Smart Balance™ Creamy Peanut Butter

"Super Great!"
-Alex Lynn age 5

"I would definitely make this."
-Lori Wells

Mock "Apple" Bars

8 cups peeled chopped zucchini
⅔ cup lemon juice
1 cup granulated sugar
1 teaspoon ground cinnamon
½ teaspoon ground nutmeg

CRUST:
4 cups GF all-purpose flour
2 cups granulated sugar
2 teaspoons xanthan gum
1 ½ cups (3 sticks) cold butter, cubed
1 teaspoon ground cinnamon

In a large saucepan over medium-low heat, cook and stir zucchini and lemon juice for 15-20 minutes or until zucchini is tender. Add sugar, cinnamon and nutmeg; simmer 1 minute longer.

Remove from heat; set aside.

Preheat oven to 375°. Grease a 15-in. x 10-in. x 1-in. baking pan.

For crust: in a medium bowl, whisk together the flour, sugar and xanthan gum; cut in butter until the mixture resembles coarse crumbs. Stir ½ cup of the crust mixture into zucchini mixture.

Press half of remaining crust mixture into prepared baking pan. Spread zucchini over top; crumble remaining crust mixture over zucchini. Sprinkle with cinnamon.

Bake for 35–40 minutes or until golden and bubbly.

Yield: 16–20 servings

"Excellent taste, I liked the cinnamon on top."
-Jonathan Holden

"Very good, tasted just like apples."
-Mary Troyer

Luscious Layered Brownies

¾ cup GF all-purpose flour
¾ cup baking cocoa
½ teaspoon xanthan gum
¼ teaspoon salt
½ cup (1 stick) butter, softened
½ cup granulated sugar
½ cup brown sugar, packed
3 eggs, *divided*
2 teaspoons vanilla extract
1 cup chopped pecans
¾ cup vanilla or white chips
½ cup caramel ice cream topping
¾ cup semi-sweet chocolate chips

Preheat oven to 350°. Grease or foil line an 8-in. square baking pan.

In a medium bowl, whisk together first four ingredients; set aside.

In a large mixing bowl, cream together butter and sugars. Add 2 eggs, one at a time, beating well after each addition. Mix in vanilla. Gradually beat in flour mixture.

Reserve ¾ cup batter; spread remaining batter into prepared baking pan. Sprinkle pecans and white chips over batter. Drizzle caramel topping over top.

Beat remaining egg into reserved batter until light in color; stir in chocolate chips. Spread evenly over caramel topping.

Bake for 30–35 minutes. Cool and cut into squares.

Yield: 12–16 servings

"Good enough to sell in a coffee shop!"
—Diane Hoehne

> "A diet is a selection of food that makes other people lose weight."
> —Unknown

Gluten-Free Breads & Muffins

breads/muffins 57

Pumpkin Cranberry Bread

1 ¼ cup GF all-purpose flour
1 cup granulated sugar
¾ teaspoon xanthan gum
1 teaspoon baking soda
½ teaspoon salt
½ teaspoon ground cinnamon
½ teaspoon ground nutmeg
1 cup canned pumpkin
½ cup canola oil
2 eggs, lightly beaten
⅜ cup buttermilk*
½ teaspoon butter flavoring
½ teaspoon pure vanilla extract
½ cup dried cranberries

Preheat oven to 350°. Grease 4 small loaf pans, 5 ¾-in. x 3-in.

In a large bowl, whisk together first seven ingredients.

In a medium bowl, whisk together the next six ingredients; stir into the dry ingredients just until moistened. Fold in the cranberries.

Spoon batter into prepared loaf pans. Bake for 35–40 minutes or until a toothpick inserted near the center comes out clean.

Cool for 10 minutes before removing from pans to wire racks to cool completely.

Yield: 4 small loaves

*See Helpful Hints

"We liked this very much. Nice and moist, great combination of taste."
-Phyllis and Joe Calle

"I love it! Can't wait to make my own!"
-Angela Yoder

Cherry Chip Muffins

1 ½ cups GF all-purpose flour
½ cup granulated sugar
2 teaspoons baking powder
1 ⅛ teaspoon xanthan gum
½ teaspoon salt
1 egg
½ cup milk*
¼ cup vegetable oil
1 jar (10 ounce) red maraschino cherries
¾ cup miniature semi-sweet chocolate chips
½ cup chopped pecans
1 cup powdered sugar

Preheat oven to 375°. Grease or paper-line miniature 24-cup muffin pan.

In a bowl, whisk together first five ingredients.

In another bowl, whisk egg, milk and oil; stir into dry ingredients just until moistened.

Drain cherries, reserving juice for glaze. Chop cherries; fold into batter with chocolate chips and pecans. Spoon the batter by the tablespoonfuls into prepared pan.

Bake for 10–13 minutes or until a toothpick inserted in the center comes out clean. Cool for 10 minutes; remove from pans to wire racks.

Combine powdered sugar and cherry juice to make a thin glaze; drizzle over muffins.

Yield: 24 mini muffins

*Recipe was tested using fat free milk

"I liked the cherries and chocolate! Awesome!"
-Jessica Brown 14 yrs. old

"I loved the cherries and chocolate chip flavor combination."
-Barb Lawrence

breads/muffins 60

"Don't change a thing—this is perfection! Especially with a cup of coffee!
-Martha Shetler

Zucchini Bread with Brown Sugar Glaze

"I liked everything about this!"
-Relva Blackstone

3 eggs
2 cups granulated sugar
1 cup vegetable oil
2 teaspoons vanilla extract
2 cups grated zucchini
1 can (8 ounces) crushed pineapple, drained
3 cups GF all-purpose flour
2 ¼ teaspoons xanthan gum
2 teaspoons baking soda
1 ½ teaspoons ground cinnamon
1 teaspoon salt
¾ teaspoon ground nutmeg
½ teaspoon baking powder
1 cup chopped walnuts

Grease five small loaf pans, 5 ¾-in. x 3-in or two loaf pans, 9-in. x 5-in. Preheat oven to 325°.

In a large bowl, beat eggs; add sugar, oil and vanilla, mix well. Stir in zucchini and pineapple.

In a separate bowl, whisk together next seven ingredients. Add to zucchini mixture and mix well with a spoon.

Pour batter into prepared loaf pans. Bake for 45–50 minutes for small loaf pans or 60–65 minutes for large loaf pans or until a toothpick inserted near the center comes out clean. Cool in pans 15 minutes before removing and cooling completely on wire racks.

BROWN SUGAR GLAZE
¼ cup butter
¼ cup granulated sugar
¼ cup packed brown sugar
¼ cup heavy whipping cream
⅔ cup powdered sugar
1 teaspoon vanilla extract

Combine first four ingredients in saucepan. Cook over medium heat until sugar is dissolved. Remove from heat and cool for 20 minutes.

Stir in powdered sugar and vanilla until smooth. Drizzle over cooled loaves.

Coconut Biscuits

2 cups GF all-purpose flour
2 tablespoons plus 1 teaspoon granulated sugar
2 ½ teaspoons baking powder
1 teaspoon xanthan gum
½ teaspoon salt
⅓ cup shortening*
1 cup milk**
½ teaspoon vanilla extract
¾ cup flaked coconut, toasted

To toast coconut: Spread shredded coconut in a thin layer on a baking sheet. Bake at 300° for about 10-15 minutes, stirring every 5 minutes to make sure that the coconut browns evenly. Remove from oven and cool.

Turn oven temperature to 425°. Grease baking sheets.

In a large bowl, whisk together the first five ingredients; cut in shortening until crumbly.

In a 1-cup measuring cup for liquids, combine milk and vanilla; stir into dry ingredients just until moistened. Fold in coconut. Drop by 2 tablespoonfuls 2 inches apart onto prepared baking sheets.

Bake for 8–10 minutes or until golden brown.

Serve warm.

Yield: 1–1 ½ dozen

*Recipe was tested using organic shortening
**Recipe was tested using fat free milk

> "I am not a coconut person, but I liked this. The texture was excellent. Jacob (12 yr. old) even liked it!"
> –Nancy Bowman

> "Mild, sweet flavor, not too sweet. Excellent with herbal tea!"
> –Eunice Hornsby

Chive 'n Cheddar Potato Muffins

2 cups milk*
¾ cup instant mashed potatoes**
1 egg
⅓ cup vegetable oil
1 cup (4 ounces) shredded cheddar cheese
1 ⅔ cups GF all-purpose flour
3 tablespoons granulated sugar
2 tablespoons snipped chives
1 tablespoons dried parsley flakes
1 tablespoon baking powder
1 ½ teaspoons xanthan gum
1 teaspoon salt

Preheat oven to 400°. Grease 12-cup muffin pan.

In a saucepan, bring milk to a boil.

Remove from the heat; stir in potato flakes. Let stand for 2 minutes. Whip with a fork until smooth; cool slightly. Beat in egg, oil and cheese.

In a medium bowl, whisk together the remaining ingredients; stir into potato mixture just until moistened (batter will be thick). Fill prepared muffin cups three-fourths full.

Bake for 15–20 minutes or until muffins test done. Cool for 5 minutes; remove from pan to a wire rack. Serve warm.

Yield: 1 Dozen

*Recipe was tested using fat free milk

**Recipe was tested using Paradise Valley All Natural, Natural Mash® instant potatoes. You may need to use less or more water depending on the type of instant potato or potato flakes you use.

"I liked the firmness, potato taste and slight saltiness. Very enjoyable, especially considering there is no gluten!"
—Ken Schloemer

Sweet Potato Biscuits

2 ½ cups GF all-purpose flour, plus flour for kneading dough
2 tablespoons granulated sugar
1 tablespoon baking powder
1 ¼ teaspoon xanthan gum
1 teaspoon ground cinnamon
1 teaspoon salt
⅓ cup shortening*
1 can (15 ounces) sweet potatoes, drained
¾ cup milk**

Preheat oven to 425°.

In a bowl whisk together the first five ingredients. Cut in shortening until mixture resembles coarse crumbs.

In a separate bowl, mash the sweet potatoes and milk. Add to the crumb mixture just until combined.

Place dough onto a floured surface; knead 8–10 times. Roll to ½-in. thickness; cut with a 2 ½-in. biscuit cutter.

Place on ungreased baking sheets. Bake for 8–10 minutes or until golden brown. Remove to wire racks. Serve warm with butter and/or honey

Yield: 15 biscuits

*Recipe was tested using organic shortening
**Recipe was tested using fat free milk

> "Great product—never had sweet potato biscuits... baked with perfection."
> –Grace Raber

Pumpkin Muffins with Chocolate Chips

2 cups GF all-purpose flour
2 ½ teaspoons baking powder
1 ½ teaspoons xanthan gum
1 teaspoon ground ginger
1 teaspoon ground cinnamon
¾ teaspoon salt
¼ teaspoon baking soda
¼ teaspoon ground allspice
1 egg
¾ cup packed brown sugar
¾ cup canned pumpkin
⅔ cup milk*
3 tablespoons butter, melted
1 teaspoon vanilla extract
½ cup semi-sweet chocolate chips

Preheat oven to 375°. Grease or paper-line 12-cup muffin pan.

In a large bowl, whisk together the first eight ingredients.

In a separate bowl combine the egg, brown sugar, pumpkin, milk, butter and vanilla; stir into dry ingredients just until moistened. Stir in chocolate chips. Fill muffin cups three-fourths full. Bake for 18–22 minutes or until a toothpick comes out clean. Cool for 5 minutes before removing from the pan to a wire rack.

Yield: 1 dozen

*Recipe was tested using fat free milk

> "Oh my gosh! Awesome!! Don't change a thing—wonderful pumpkin flavor with a hint of chocolate!"
> –Toni Weaver

Cherry Pecan Bread

½ cup (1 stick) butter, softened
¾ cup granulated sugar
2 eggs
2 cups GF all-purpose flour
1 ½ teaspoons xanthan gum
1 teaspoon baking soda
½ teaspoon salt
1 cup buttermilk*
1 cup chopped pecans
1 jar (10 ounces) maraschino cherries, drained and chopped
1 teaspoon vanilla extract

Preheat oven to 350°.

Grease 4 small loaf pans, 5 ¾-in. x 3-in.

In a mixing bowl, cream the butter and sugar. Add eggs, one at a time, beating well after each addition.

Whisk together the next 4 ingredients. Add to the creamed mixture alternately with buttermilk. Stir in the pecans, cherries and vanilla. Pour into prepared loaf pans.

Bake for 35–40 minutes or until a toothpick inserted near the center comes out clean.

Cool for 10 minutes before removing from the pan to a wire rack.

Yield: 4 mini loaves

*See Helpful Hints

"This was excellent—the texture, flavor, everything! I certainly did not miss the gluten!"
-Kathy Whitley

65 breads/muffins

Apple-Praline Bread

1–1 ¼ cups chopped pecans, *divided*
1 (8 ounce) container sour cream*
1 cup granulated sugar
2 large eggs
1 tablespoon pure vanilla extract
2 cups GF all-purpose flour
2 teaspoons baking powder
1 ½ teaspoons xanthan gum
½ teaspoon baking soda
½ teaspoon salt
½ teaspoon cinnamon
1 ½ cups finely chopped, peeled tart apples
½ cup butter
½ cup firmly packed brown sugar

Preheat oven to 350°. Bake ½ cup pecans in a single layer in a shallow pan 6–8 minutes or until toasted and fragrant, stirring after 3-4 minutes. While pecans are baking, grease 4 small loaf pans, 5 ¾-in. x 3-in. In a large mixing bowl, beat next four ingredients at low speed for 2 minutes or until blended. In a separate bowl, whisk together next six ingredients. Add to sour cream mixture, beating until just blended. Stir in apples and ½ cup toasted pecans.

Spoon batter into prepared loaf pans. Sprinkle with remaining ½–¾ cup chopped pecans, lightly press pecans into batter. Bake for 35–40 minutes or until a toothpick inserted near the center comes out clean. Loosely cover bread with aluminum foil after 20 minutes to prevent excessive browning. Cool in pan on a wire rack for 10 minutes before removing bread from pan to cool on rack completely.

While bread is cooling, bring butter and brown sugar to a boil in a 1-qt. heavy saucepan over medium heat, stirring constantly; boil 1 minute. Remove from heat, and spoon over top of bread; let cool completely.

Yield: 4 small loaves

*Recipe was tested with light sour cream

> "Wonderful! Taste a little like candy apples!"
> -Rose Eby
>
> "Very moist, liked the topping. From the ones I have tasted, this is the best!"
> -Erma Beachy

Chocolate Chip Muffins

½ cup (1 stick) butter, softened
1 cup granulated sugar
2 eggs
1 cup (8 ounces) vanilla yogurt
1 teaspoon vanilla extract
2 cups GF all-purpose flour
1 ½ teaspoons xanthan gum
1 teaspoon baking soda
½ teaspoon baking powder
½ teaspoon salt
¾ cup semi-sweet chocolate chips

TOPPING:
¼ cup semi-sweet chocolate chips
2 tablespoons brown sugar
2 tablespoons chopped walnuts, optional
1 teaspoon ground cinnamon

Preheat oven to 350°. Grease or paper-line a 12-cup muffin pan.

In a large bowl, cream butter and sugar. Add eggs, one at a time, beating well after each addition. Add yogurt and vanilla; mix well.

In a separate bowl, whisk together next five ingredients. Stir into creamed mixture just until moistened. Fold in chocolate chips. Fill prepared muffin cups two-thirds full.

Combine topping ingredients; sprinkle over batter.

Bake for 15–20 minutes or until a toothpick inserted near the center comes out clean.

Cool for 5 minutes before removing from the pans to wire racks.

Yield: 1 Dozen

"It was *INCREDIBLE*. I told my mom I could have eaten 10 they were so good!"
—Bryan Tesh

"They were some of the best dang muffins I've ever had!"
—Lisa White

"Excellent taste and texture—we liked these!"
-Tracey Troyer

Squash Muffins

1 pound yellow summer squash, cut into 1-in. slices
½ cup (1 stick) butter, melted
1 egg, lightly beaten
1 ½ cups GF all-purpose flour
½ cup granulated sugar
2 ½ teaspoons baking powder
1 ⅛ teaspoons xanthan gum
½ teaspoon salt

Preheat oven to 375°. Grease a 12-cup muffin pan. Place 1 in. of water in a saucepan; add squash. Bring to a boil, reduce heat, cover and simmer for 15–20 minutes or until tender. Drain well and mash. Measure enough squash to equal 1 cup. Combine squash, butter and egg; stir well and set aside. In a separate bowl, whisk together remaining ingredients; stir in squash mixture until just moistened. Fill prepared muffin cups three-fourths full.

Bake for 20–25 minutes or until toothpick inserted near the center comes out clean. Cool for 5 minutes before removing from pan to a wire rack.

Yield: 1 dozen

*These muffins are best warm from the oven. If there are any left over, freeze them, then reheat them in the microwave.

Peach Muffins

1 ½ cups GF all-purpose flour
1 cup granulated sugar
1 ⅛ teaspoons xanthan gum
¾ teaspoon salt
½ teaspoon baking soda
¼ rounded teaspoon ground cinnamon
2 eggs
½ cup vegetable oil
½ teaspoon vanilla extract
1 can (15 ¼ ounces) sliced peaches*, drained and finely chopped

Preheat oven to 350°. Grease or paper-line 12 cup muffin pan.

In a large bowl, whisk together the first six ingredients.

In a separate bowl, whisk the eggs, oil and vanilla; stir into dry ingredients just until moistened (batter will be thick). Fold in peaches. Fill prepared muffin cups two-thirds full.

Bake for 15–20 minutes or until a toothpick inserted in the center comes out clean.

Cool for 5 minutes before removing from pan to a wire rack

Yield: 1 dozen

*Use a food processor or blender to chop peaches easily

"I liked everything about this muffin, especially the tender crumb texture. Just the right amount of sweetness and moistness."
-Ilana Erwin

Chocolate Banana-Nut Bread

½ cup (1 stick) butter, softened
1 cup granulated sugar
2 eggs
1 cup mashed ripe bananas (about 2 medium)
¼ cup milk*
1 teaspoon vanilla extract
2 cups GF all-purpose flour
⅓ cup baking cocoa
1 ½ teaspoons xanthan gum
1 teaspoon baking soda
1 teaspoon salt
½ cup chopped nuts

Preheat oven to 350°. Grease one 9-in. x 5-in. loaf pan or four 5 ¾-in. x 3-in. mini loaf pans.

In a mixing bowl, cream butter and sugar. Add eggs, bananas, milk and vanilla; mix well.

In a separate bowl, whisk together next 5 ingredients. Add to the banana mixture and mix until just combined. Fold in nuts. Spoon into prepared pan(s).

Bake for 60–65 minutes for large loaf or 40-45 minutes for mini loaves, or until a toothpick inserted near the center comes out clean.

Cool for 10 minutes before removing from pan to a wire rack.

Yield: 1 large loaf or 4 mini loaves

*Recipe was tested using fat free milk

> "An excellent blend of chocolate and banana. Moist and delicious."
> -Eunice Hornsby

> "Not as heavy as banana bread can be – just the right amount of chocolate – can still taste the bananas. I would make this!"
> -Kathy Whitley

"Tastes just like regular corn bread."
-Kristen Eckstein

Corn Bread

1 ¼ cups GF all-purpose flour
¾ cup corn meal
¼ cup granulated sugar
2 teaspoons baking powder
¾ teaspoon xanthan gum
½ teaspoon salt
1 cup milk*
¼ cup vegetable oil
1 egg, beaten

Preheat oven to 400°. Grease an 8-in. or 9-in. square baking pan.

In a medium bowl, whisk together the first six ingredients.

In a small bowl, combine the milk, oil and egg; stir into dry ingredients mixing just until moistened. Pour batter into prepared pan.

Bake 20–25 minutes or until light golden brown and wooden toothpick inserted in center comes out clean. Serve warm.

Yield: 9 servings

*Recipe was tested using fat free milk

Dill Drop Biscuits

2 cups GF all-purpose flour
1 tablespoons baking powder
2–3 teaspoons dill weed
1 teaspoon xanthan gum
¾ teaspoon salt
¼ teaspoon pepper
½ cup (1 stick) cold butter
2 eggs, lightly beaten
½ cup plus 1 tablespoon half-an-half cream, *divided*

Preheat oven to 450°.

In a medium bowl, whisk together the first six ingredients.

Cut in butter until mixture resembles coarse crumbs.

With a fork, stir in eggs and ½ cup cream just until moistened.

Drop by ¼ cupfuls onto an ungreased baking sheet. Brush tops with remaining cream.

Bake for 10–12 minutes or until golden brown.

Serve warm with butter.

Yield: 1 dozen

"I didn't notice any taste difference compared to regular flour. These would go well with soup, chicken or fish."
-Sue Spessard

Apple Streusel Muffins

2 cups GF all-purpose flour
1 cup granulated sugar
1 ½ teaspoons xanthan gum
1 teaspoon ground cinnamon
1 teaspoon baking powder
½ teaspoon ground nutmeg
½ teaspoon baking soda
½ teaspoon salt
2 eggs
½ cup (1 stick) butter, melted
1 ¼ teaspoons vanilla extract
1 ½ cups peeled, chopped tart apples

STREUSEL TOPPING:
⅓ cup packed brown sugar
1 tablespoon GF all-purpose flour
¼ teaspoon ground cinnamon
1 tablespoon cold butter

Preheat oven to 375°. Grease or paper-line 12-cup muffin pan.

In a large mixing bowl, whisk together first eight ingredients.

In a small mixing bowl, whisk the eggs, butter and vanilla; stir into dry ingredients just until moistened (batter will be stiff). Fold in apples.

Fill prepared muffin cups ¾ full.

In a small bowl, combine the brown sugar, flour and cinnamon; cut in butter until crumbly. Sprinkle over batter.

Bake for 15–20 minutes or until a toothpick inserted near the center comes out clean. Cool for 5 minutes before removing from pan to wire rack to cool completely.

Yield: 1 dozen

"I loved everything about it!! This is definitely one recipe I want to use!"
-Martha Shetler

"Excellent taste and texture—my favorite item yet!"
-Rhoda Hochstetler

Cream Cheese Filled Carrot Muffins

1 can (15 ounces) sliced carrots, drained
1 ¾ cups GF all-purpose flour
1 cup granulated sugar
1 ¼ teaspoon baking soda
1 ⅛ teaspoon xanthan gum
½ teaspoon salt
½ teaspoon ground cinnamon
⅛ teaspoon ground allspice
⅛ teaspoon ground cloves
⅛ teaspoon ground nutmeg
1 egg
⅓ cup canola oil

FILLING:
2 packages (3 ounces) cream cheese, softened
1 egg
3 tablespoons granulated sugar

Preheat oven to 350°. Grease a 12-cup muffin pan.

Place carrots in a food processor; cover and process until smooth.

In a large bowl, whisk together the next nine ingredients.

In a small bowl, whisk the pureed carrots, egg and oil; stir into the dry ingredients just until moistened. Fill muffin cups one-third full. Using a small cookie scoop or spoon, create a well in dough.

In a small bowl, beat the filling ingredients until smooth. Drop by tablespoonfuls into the center of each muffin. Top with remaining batter.

Bake for 20–25 minutes or until a toothpick comes out clean.

Cool for 5 minutes before removing from pan to a wire rack.

Yield: 1 dozen

"Very moist—I liked the taste of the spices."
  -Ann Holden

"Not too sweet, nice balance of cheese and carrots."
  -Audrey Stein

Secret Chocolate Muffins

½ cup (1 stick) butter, softened
1 cup granulated sugar
2 eggs
1 teaspoon vanilla extract
1 ½ cups GF all-purpose flour
4 tablespoons baking cocoa
1 ⅛ teaspoon xanthan gum
½ teaspoon salt
½ teaspoon baking soda
½ teaspoon ground cinnamon
1 cup grated green tomato*
½ cup semi-sweet chocolate chips

Preheat oven to 350°. Grease a 12-cup muffin pan.

In a large mixing bowl, cream the butter and sugar. Beat in eggs and vanilla.

In a separate bowl, whisk together the next six ingredients; gradually add to creamed mixture. Stir in the green tomato and chocolate chips. Fill muffin cups ⅔ full.

Bake for 20–25 minutes or until a toothpick inserted near the center comes out clean. Cool for 10 minutes before removing from pan to wire rack.

Yield: 1 dozen

*Grated zucchini may be substituted for the green tomato

Serving suggestion: Serve warm with a scoop of your favorite ice cream!

This recipe is one great way to use up those left over green tomatoes from your garden at the end of the growing season! Just grate tomatoes in food processor, measure, and place in freezer safe containers. Don't forget to label and date the container. You may have to drain some of the liquid before using in a recipe.

"Very moist, very nice amount of chocolate. Joshua, age 3—ate almost half by himself—a good sign that he really liked it!"
-Michelle Robirds

"Great chocolatey taste, all around excellent!"
-Brian Rohrig

Spiced Blueberry Muffins

1 ¾ cups GF all-purpose flour
½ cup granulated sugar
2 ½ teaspoons baking powder
1 ¼ teaspoons xanthan gum
1 rounded teaspoon ground cinnamon
½ teaspoon salt
¼ teaspoon ground nutmeg
1 egg, lightly beaten
¾ cup milk*
⅓ cup (5 ⅓ tablespoons) butter, melted
1 ¼ cups fresh or frozen blueberries**

TOPPING:
1 tablespoon sugar
½ teaspoon ground cinnamon

Preheat oven to 400°. Grease or paper-line a 12-cup muffin pan.

In a large bowl, whisk together first seven ingredients.

In separate bowl, combine egg and milk. Add egg mixture and butter to dry ingredients; stir just until moistened. Fold in blueberries. Fill prepared muffin cups two-thirds full.

Combine topping ingredients; sprinkle over batter.

Bake for 15–20 minutes or until a toothpick comes out clean.

Cool for 5 minutes before removing from pan to a wire rack.

Yield: 1 dozen

*This recipe was tested using fat free milk
**If using frozen blueberries, do not thaw before adding to batter

> "I liked the cinnamon and spiced flavor. It was really good."
> –Payton Ikels, age 9
>
> "When I warmed it up and ate it, it was very moist and delicious."
> –Ben Drumm

Pumpkin Ginger Scones

2 cups GF all-purpose flour
7 tablespoons granulated sugar
2 teaspoons baking powder
1 teaspoon ground cinnamon
¾ teaspoon xanthan gum
½ teaspoon salt
½ teaspoon ground ginger
¼ teaspoon baking soda
5 tablespoons cold butter, *divided*
1 egg, lightly beaten
¼ cup canned pumpkin
¼ cup sour cream*
1 teaspoon granulated sugar

Preheat oven to 425°. Grease baking sheet.

In a large bowl, whisk together the first eight ingredients. Cut in 4 tablespoons butter until mixture resembles coarse crumbs.

In a separate bowl, combine the egg, pumpkin and sour cream; stir into crumb mixture just until moistened.

Turn onto a floured surface; knead 10 times.

Pat into an 8-in. circle on baking sheet. Cut into eight wedges. Slightly separate wedges.

Melt remaining butter; brush over dough. Sprinkle with remaining sugar.

Bake for 15–20 minutes or until golden brown.

Serve warm.

Yield: 8 scones

*These are also good using vanilla yogurt instead of the sour cream.

> "Loved the pumpkin flavor!! Great fall breakfast treat!"
> —Toni Weaver

Raspberry Chip Muffins

1 cup frozen raspberries
¾ cup plus 2 tablespoons granulated sugar, *divided*
¼ (½ stick) cup butter, softened
1 egg
½ teaspoon almond extract
½ teaspoon vanilla extract
2 ¼ cups GF all-purpose flour
1 tablespoon baking powder
1 ⅝ teaspoons xanthan gum
½ teaspoon salt
1 cup half-and-half
½ cup vanilla or white chips
2 tablespoons brown sugar

Preheat oven to 375°. Grease or paper-line a 12-cup muffin pan.

In a small bowl, toss raspberries with ¼ cup sugar; set aside.

In a large mixing bowl, cream butter and ½ cup sugar. Beat in egg and extracts.

In a separated bowl, whisk together the next four ingredients. Add to creamed mixture alternately with cream. Fold in vanilla chips and raspberries. Fill prepared muffin pan three-fourths full.

Combine brown sugar and remaining remaining sugar; sprinkle over batter.

Bake for 20–25 minutes or until a toothpick inserted in center of muffin comes out clean.

Cool for 5 minutes before removing from pan to a wire rack. Serve warm, with or without butter.

Yield: 1 dozen

"I liked the flavor of these muffins. They had excellent taste and texture—healthy and delicious."

-Riti Joshi, age 11

Berries 'n Cream Coffee Cake

¼ cup (½ stick) butter, softened
⅔ cup granulated sugar
1 egg
1 cup plus 2 tablespoons GF all-purpose flour, *divided*
½ teaspoon xanthan gum
½ teaspoon ground cinnamon
½ teaspoon baking powder
¼ teaspoon salt
½ cup milk*
1 cup fresh or frozen blueberries**
1 package (3 ounces) cream cheese***, cubed

TOPPING:
2 tablespoons GF all-purpose flour
2 tablespoons granulated sugar
1 tablespoon cold butter

Preheat oven to 375°. Grease 8-in. square baking dish.

For batter, in a large mixing bowl, cream butter and sugar. Beat in egg.

In a separate bowl, whisk together 1 cup flour and next four ingredients; gradually add to creamed mixture alternately with milk.

Toss blueberries with remaining flour. Stir blueberries and cream cheese into creamed mixture (batter will be thick). Transfer into prepared baking dish.

For topping, in a small bowl, combine flour and sugar. Cut in butter until crumbly. Sprinkle over batter.

Bake for 40–45 minutes or until a toothpick inserted near the center comes out clean.

Cool on a wire rack.

Yield: 6–8 servings

*Recipe was tested using fat-free milk
**If using frozen blueberries, do not thaw before adding to batter
***Recipe was tested using light cream cheese

"Wow! This is amazing!"
-Girija Parvate

"I was tempted not to eat it because I was under the impression that gluten-free equals dry and nasty, but I was completely mistaken. These were delicious!"
-Lisa Chapman

Vanilla French Toast

1 cup milk*
1 package (3 ounce) cook-and-serve vanilla pudding mix
1 egg
½ teaspoon ground cinnamon**
24 slices GF pecan-cinnamon bread*** (½ inch thick)
Butter or oil

In a bowl, whisk the milk, pudding mix, egg and cinnamon for 2 minutes or until well blended.

Dip bread in pudding mixture, coating both sides.

Brush oil or melt butter on hot griddle; cook French toast for 2–4 minutes on each side or until golden brown.

Yield: 8–12 servings

*Recipe was tested using fat-free milk
**This recipe was tested using a bit more cinnamon (rounded or heaping spoonful) than a level spoonful.
***This recipe was tested using "Bette's Four Flour Bread" recipe from *The Gluten-Free Gourmet Bakes Bread* by Bette Hagman, the cinnamon-nut variation.

"Loved this recipe. Bread was not too heavy or dense. The nuts were a great addition."
-Grooms Family

"The flavor was wonderful— as good as my own! I love the cinnamon in it."
-Barb Lawrence

Gingerbread Pancakes

1 cup GF all-purpose flour
2 tablespoons granulated sugar
1 teaspoon baking powder
½ teaspoon xanthan gum
½ teaspoon (heaping) ground cinnamon
¼ teaspoon ground ginger
¼ teaspoon ground allspice
1 egg
¾ cup milk*
2 tablespoons molasses
1 tablespoon vegetable oil

In a large bowl, whisk together the first seven ingredients.

In a separate bowl, combine the egg, milk, molasses and oil; stir into dry ingredients just until moistened.

Pour batter by ¼ cupfuls onto a greased hot griddle**; turn when bubbles form on top.

Cook until the second side is golden brown.

Watch carefully, these brown up fast.

 Serve with maple syrup.

Options: may add dried fruit or nuts to batter before cooking.

Yield: 4–6 Servings

*Recipe was tested using fat-free milk
**If using a non-stick griddle, no need to oil or grease cooking surface.

Pineapple Coffee Cake

1 cup granulated sugar
½ cup vegetable oil
2 eggs
1 cup (8 ounces) sour cream*
1 ½ cups GF all-purpose flour
2 teaspoons baking powder
¾ teaspoon xanthan gum
½ teaspoon ground cinnamon
½ teaspoon salt
1 can (8 ounces) crushed pineapple, drained

TOPPING:
½ cup flaked coconut
⅓ cup chopped walnuts (optional)
3 tablespoons sugar
½ teaspoon ground cinnamon

Preheat oven to 350°. Grease a 9-inch square baking pan.

In a mixing bowl, blend the sugar and oil. Add eggs, one at a time, beating well after each addition. Beat in the sour cream.

In separate bowl, whisk together the next five ingredients. Add to the sour cream mixture. Stir in the pineapple. Spoon batter into prepared pan.

In a small bowl, combine the topping ingredients; sprinkle over batter.

Bake for 35–40 minutes or until a toothpick inserted near center comes out clean.

Cool on wire rack.

Yield: 9 servings

*Recipe was tested using light sour cream

"I liked the low level of sweetness and moistness. I don't know what gluten-free usually tastes like, but this was very satisfying for a sweet treat."
–Nancy Florence

"Excellent flavor!"
–Sue Spessard

Pecan Pancakes

1 ⅓ cups GF all-purpose flour
2 tablespoons granulated sugar
1 tablespoon baking powder
⅝ teaspoon xanthan gum
½ teaspoon salt
¼ teaspoon ground cinnamon
1 egg
1 cup milk*
3 tablespoons vegetable oil
½ cup chopped pecans

In a small bowl, whisk together the first 6 ingredients.

In a separate bowl, combine the egg, milk and oil.

Stir into dry ingredients just until moistened.

Fold in pecans.

Pour batter by ¼ cupfuls onto a lightly greased hot griddle**.

Turn when bubbles form on top of the pancake; cook until second side is golden brown.

Yield: 1 dozen pancakes

*Recipe was tested using fat-free milk
**If using a non-stick griddle, no need to oil or grease cooking surface.

These are excellent served with a fruity syrup!

Chocolate Chip Coffee Cake

1 cup (2 sticks) butter, softened
1 package (8 ounces) cream cheese*, softened
1 ½ cup granulated sugar, *divided*
2 eggs
1 teaspoon vanilla extract
2 cups GF all-purpose flour
1 teaspoon xanthan gum
1 teaspoon baking powder
½ teaspoon baking soda
¼ teaspoon salt
¼ cup milk**
1 cup semi-sweet chocolate chips
¼ cup chopped pecans
1 teaspoon ground cinnamon

Preheat oven to 350°. Grease 9-in. springform pan.

In a mixing bowl, cream butter, cream cheese and 1¼ cups sugar. Beat in eggs and vanilla extract.

In a separate bowl, whisk together the next five ingredients; add to creamed mixture alternately with milk. Stir in chocolate chips. Pour into prepared pan.

Combine the pecans, cinnamon and remaining sugar; sprinkle over batter.

Bake 50-55 minutes or until a toothpick inserted near the center comes out clean.

Cool for 15 minutes.

Carefully run a knife around the edge of pan to loosen. Remove sides of pan.

Cool completely before cutting.

Yield: 8–10 servings

*Recipe was tested using light cream cheese
**Recipe was tested using fat-free milk

> "I absolutely loved the moist texture! This cake was delicious through and through!"
> –Jordan Kiener

> "It was the moistest coffee cake I've ever had. Loved the texture! Very, very good."
> –Eric Holden

Baked Maple French Toast

12 slices GF bread*, cubed
1 (8ounce) package cream cheese**, cubed
8 eggs
1 cup milk***
½ cup maple syrup

Grease shallow 2-qt. baking dish.

Arrange half of the bread cubes in prepared baking dish. Top with the cream cheese and remaining bread.

In a bowl, whisk eggs, milk and syrup; pour over bread. Cover and refrigerate overnight.

Remove from the refrigerator 30 minutes before baking.

Preheat oven to 350°.

Cover and bake for 30 minutes.

Uncover; bake 20–25 minutes longer or until golden brown. Serve with additional syrup.

Yield: 8 servings

*This recipe was tested using "Bette's Four Flour Bread" recipe from *The Gluten-Free Gourmet Bakes Bread* by Bette Hagman, the cinnamon-nut variation.
**Recipe was tested using light cream cheese
***Recipe was tested using fat-free milk

Nutmeg Coffee Cake

¾ cup (1 ½ sticks) butter, softened
1 cup granulated sugar
2 eggs
2 cups GF all-purpose flour
1 teaspoon xanthan gum
1 teaspoon baking soda
1 teaspoon ground nutmeg
½ teaspoon salt
1 cup (8 ounces) sour cream*
¾ cup packed brown sugar
¾ cup chopped pecans
1 teaspoon ground cinnamon
1 ½ cups powdered sugar
3 tablespoons milk**

Grease 13-in. x 9-in. x 2-in. baking pan.

In a large mixing bowl, cream butter and sugar. Add eggs, one at a time, beating well after each addition.

In a separate bowl, whisk together the next five ingredients; add to creamed mixture alternately with sour cream. Pour into prepared baking dish.

In a small bowl, combine brown sugar, pecans and cinnamon; sprinkle over coffee cake. Cover and refrigerate overnight.

Remove from the refrigerator 30 minutes before baking.

Preheat oven to 350°.

Bake, uncovered for 35–40 minutes or until a toothpick inserted near the center comes out clean.

Cool on a wire rack for 10 minutes.

Combine powdered sugar and milk; drizzle over warm coffee cake.

Yield: 12–15 servings

*Recipe was tested using light sour cream
**Recipe was tested using fat-free milk

"The topping is very tasty—enjoyed the combination of spices, sugar and nuts. This is a great coffee cake, especially with the drizzled icing. Super when served right from the oven! Yum!"
-Jeff & Carol Kable

Coconut-Walnut Coffee Cake

1 cup vegetable oil
1 cup granulated sugar
1 cup packed brown sugar
2 eggs
1 teaspoon vanilla extract
2 ½ cups GF all-purpose flour
1 ¼ teaspoons xanthan gum
1 teaspoon baking soda
1 teaspoon salt
1 teaspoon ground cinnamon
1 cup buttermilk*
1 cup flaked coconut
1 cup chopped walnuts
Powdered sugar

Preheat oven to 350°. Grease 13-in. x 9-in. x 2-in. baking pan.

In a large mixing bowl, combine the oil, sugars, eggs and vanilla; mix well.

In a separate bowl, whisk together the next five ingredients; add to the egg mixture alternately with buttermilk. Stir just until moistened. Stir in coconut and walnuts just until combined. Pour into prepared pan.

Bake for 45–55 minutes or until toothpick inserted near the center comes out clean.

Cool on a wire rack.

Dust with powdered sugar if desired.

Yield: 12–15 servings

*See Helpful Hints

"We all loved the taste! When is this book coming out?"
–Shashank Modak

"The moist, crunchy, spicy, and nutty coffee cake had a delightful taste."
–Catherine Conte

Pumpkin Pancakes

2 cups GF all-purpose flour
2 tablespoons granulated sugar
1 tablespoon plus 1 teaspoon baking powder
1 teaspoon xanthan gum
1 teaspoon salt
1 teaspoon ground cinnamon
½ teaspoon ground nutmeg
½ teaspoon ground cloves
4 large eggs, separated
1 ½ cups milk*
1 cup canned pumpkin
½ cup (1 stick) butter, melted

In a large bowl, whisk together first eight ingredients. Make a well in center of mixture.

In a medium bowl, whisk together egg yolks and next three ingredients. Add to flour mixture, stirring just until dry ingredients are moistened – scrape sides and bottom of bowl to make sure all flour is moistened.

In a small mixing bowl, beat egg whites at high speed until stiff peaks form. Gently fold into pumpkin mixture.

Pour about ¼ cup batter for each pancake onto a hot, lightly greased griddle. If using a griddle with a non-stick coating, there will be no need to grease.

Cook pancakes until tops are covered with bubbles and edges look cooked. Turn and cook other side.

Yield: about 24 pancakes

*Recipe was tested using fat-free milk

Chocolate Cinnamon Coffee Cake

3 cups GF all-purpose flour
2 cups granulated sugar
1 cup (2 sticks) cold butter
2 tablespoons baking cocoa
1 tablespoon ground cinnamon
1 teaspoon baking soda
1 teaspoon xanthan gum
½ teaspoon baking powder
½ teaspoon ground nutmeg
⅛ teaspoon salt
⅛ teaspoon ground cloves
1 cup chopped nuts
2 cups buttermilk*

Preheat oven to 350°. Grease a 13-in. x 9-in. x 2-in. baking pan.

In a large bowl, whisk together the flour and sugar; cut in butter until crumbly. Set aside 1¼ cups for topping.

To the remaining mixture, add the next 8 ingredients. Mix well. Stir in nuts. Make a well in the center; pour in buttermilk and stir just until moistened. Pour into prepared pan.

Sprinkle with reserved crumb mixture.

Bake for 35–40 minutes or until a toothpick inserted near the center comes out clean.

Cool on a wire rack.

Yield: 12–16 servings

*See Helpful Hints

"Very nice subtle chocolate flavor. My husband, who is picky, gave it an excellent rating!"
-Miriam & Perry Beachy

"Texture is so great, I can't even tell it's gluten-free—Yay!"
-Josie Grim

Strawberry Topped- Cream Cheese Filled- French Toast

1 package (8 ounce) cream cheese*, softened
3 tablespoons powdered sugar
1 teaspoon vanilla extract
1 loaf (12 slices) GF bread**
2 eggs
1 cup milk***
2 cups sliced fresh or frozen strawberries
2 tablespoons sugar

In a small bowl, combine the cream cheese, sugar and vanilla. Spread 2 tablespoons on each of 6 slices of bread; top with remaining bread slices.

In a separate bowl, beat eggs and milk; soak sandwiches for 1–2 minutes per side.

Cook on a greased hot griddle for 5 minutes on each side or until golden brown and heated through.

While toast is cooking, place strawberries and sugar in microwave safe bowl and microwave until heated through.

Serve with strawberries.

Yield: 4–6 servings

*Recipe was tested using light cream cheese
**This recipe was tested using "Bette's Four Flour Bread" recipe from *The Gluten-Free Gourmet Bakes Bread* by Bette Hagman, the cinnamon-nut variation.
***Recipe was tested using fat-free milk

Chocolate Chip Pancakes

2 cups GF all-purpose flour
2 teaspoons granulated sugar
2 teaspoons baking powder
1 teaspoon xanthan gum
1 teaspoon baking soda
¼ teaspoon salt
2 eggs, lightly beaten
2 cups buttermilk*
¼ cup vegetable oil
1 cup miniature semi-sweet chocolate chips

In a bowl, whisk together first six ingredients.

In a small bowl, combine the eggs, buttermilk and oil; stir into dry ingredients just until moistened.

Pour the batter by ¼ cupfuls onto a greased hot griddle**.

Sprinkle each pancake with 2 teaspoons chocolate chips.

Turn when bubbles form on top of pancake; cook until second side is golden brown.

Yield: 6–8 servings

*See Helpful Hints

**If using a non-stick griddle, no need to oil or grease cooking surface.

Apple Pecan Pancakes

1 cup GF all-purpose flour
½ cup granulated sugar
1 teaspoon baking powder
¾ teaspoon cinnamon
½ teaspoon xanthan gum
½ teaspoon baking soda
½ teaspoon ground nutmeg
¼ teaspoon ground ginger
¼ teaspoon ground cloves
¼ teaspoon salt
1 egg
¾ cup plus 2 tablespoons buttermilk*
1 ½ tablespoons vegetable oil
1 cup chopped peeled apples
½ cup chopped pecans

In a large bowl, whisk together first ten ingredients.

In a separate bowl, combine the egg, buttermilk and oil; stir into the dry ingredients just until blended.

Stir in apples and pecans.

Pour the batter by ¼ cupfuls onto a greased griddle** over medium-low heat.

Turn when bubbles form on top; cook until second side is golden brown.

Yield: 4–5 servings

*See Helpful Hints

**If using a non-stick griddle, no need to oil or grease cooking surface.

Toffee-Topped Coffee Cake

2 cups GF all-purpose flour
1 cup packed brown sugar
½ cup granulated sugar
½ cup (1 stick) cold butter
1 teaspoon xanthan gum
1 teaspoon baking soda
1 teaspoon salt
1 egg
1 cup buttermilk*
1 teaspoon vanilla extract
½ cup toffee bits
½ cup chocolate chips
1 cup chopped pecans

Preheat oven to 350°. Grease an 11-in. x 7-in. x 2-in. baking pan.

In a large bowl, whisk together the flour and sugars; cut in butter until the mixture resembles coarse crumbs. Set aside ½ cup for topping.

To the remaining crumb mixture, add xanthan gum, baking soda and salt.

In a small mixing bowl, beat egg, buttermilk and vanilla; add to the crumb mixture and mix well. Pour into a greased 11-in. x 7-in. x 2-in. baking pan.

Combine the toffee bits, chocolate chips, pecans and reserved crumb mixture; sprinkle over the top.

Bake for 40 minutes or until a toothpick inserted near the center comes out clean.

Yield: 8–10 servings

*See Helpful Hints

"Wow! That's incredible! That's gluten-free? That's outstanding!"
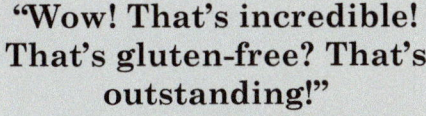
-David Grissom

"Mmmmm good! I want the recipe!"
-Kelli

Blueberry Brunch Casserole

8 slices GF bread*, cut into ½-inch cubes
1 ½ cup blueberries, fresh or frozen
12 ounces cream cheese, softened
8 eggs
½ cup vanilla or plain yogurt
⅓ cup sour cream**
1 teaspoon vanilla extract
¾ teaspoon ground cinnamon
½ cup milk***
⅓ cup maple syrup
Additional blueberries, optional
Additional maple syrup

Grease a shallow 3-qt. baking dish.

Place half of the bread cubes in prepared baking dish. Sprinkle with blueberries.

In a mixing bowl, beat cream cheese until smooth. Beat in the eggs, yogurt, sour cream, vanilla and cinnamon. Gradually add milk and syrup until blended.

Pour half over the bread. Top with the remaining bread and cream cheese mixture. Cover and refrigerate overnight.

Remove from the refrigerator 30 minutes before baking. Preheat oven to 350°. Cover and bake for 30 minutes. Uncover; bake 20–25 minutes longer or until a knife inserted near the center comes out clean.

Sprinkle with additional blueberries if desired. Let stand for 5 minutes. Serve with syrup.

Yield: 6–8 servings

*This recipe was tested using "Bette's Four Flour Bread" recipe from *The Gluten-Free Gourmet Bakes Bread* by Bette Hagman, the cinnamon-nut variation.

**Recipe was tested using light sour cream

***Recipe was tested using fat-free milk

Walnut-Cranberry Baked French Toast

1 loaf GF bread*, ½ inch slices
4 tablespoons butter, melted
½ cup chopped walnuts
½ cup cranberries
6 eggs
1 cup milk**
⅓ cup packed brown sugar
1 teaspoon ground nutmeg
¼ teaspoon salt
1 teaspoon vanilla extract

Line the bottom of a greased 8-inch square baking dish with a single layer of bread slices, making sure they fit snugly, cutting them if necessary.

Brush bread layer with some of the butter, then sprinkle with half of the walnuts and cranberries. Top with a second layer of bread and brush with butter. Sprinkle remaining walnuts and cranberries.

In a medium bowl, whisk together remaining ingredients. Pour mixture over bread, making sure to soak the top layer completely. Cover and refrigerate overnight.

When ready to bake, remove pan from refrigerator and let sit at room temperature for 30 minutes.

Preheat oven to 350°.

Uncover and bake until golden brown and cooked through, about 45 minutes. Set aside for 5–10 minutes then serve.

Yield: 4–6 servings

*This recipe was tested using "Bette's Four Flour Bread" recipe from *The Gluten-Free Gourmet Bakes Bread* by Bette Hagman, the cinnamon variation.

**Recipe was tested using fat-free milk

Plan ahead! Needs to refrigerate overnight.

Strawberry-Pecan Coffee Cake

1 cup GF all-purpose flour
½ cup granulated sugar
2 teaspoons baking powder
½ teaspoon salt
½ teaspoon xanthan gum
¼ teaspoon ground cinnamon
¼ teaspoon ground nutmeg
1 egg
½ cup buttermilk*
2 tablespoons butter, melted
1 ½ cup sliced fresh strawberries

TOPPING:
½ cup GF all-purpose flour
½ cup granulated sugar
¼ cup (½ stick) cold butter
½ cup chopped pecans

Preheat oven to 375°. Grease 8-in. square baking dish.

In a large bowl, whisk together the first seven ingredients.

In another bowl, combine the egg, buttermilk and butter; stir into dry ingredients just until moistened. Pour into prepared baking dish. Top with strawberries.

For topping, combine flour and sugar in a bowl; cut in butter until crumbly. Stir in pecans; sprinkle over strawberries.

Bake for 30–35 minutes or until a toothpick inserted near the center comes out clean.

Cut into squares.

Yield: 9 servings

*See Helpful Hints

"We all loved the taste! Very good. 2 thumbs up!"
-George Hamlin

"Very good. I don't think you can tell it's supposed to be good for you!"
-Teri Hamlin

Gluten-Free Entrees

"The only time to eat diet food is while you're waiting for the steak to cook."
 -Julia Childs

Creamed Chicken over Rice

4 boneless, skinless chicken breasts, cubed
Lemon pepper
2 cups instant brown rice
1 ½ cup milk*
2 tablespoons butter
2 tablespoons GF all-purpose flour
1 teaspoon salt
Dash pepper
Hot cooked rice

Place chicken in skillet, sprinkle with lemon pepper and brown.

While chicken is browning, cook rice according to package directions.

Meanwhile, melt butter in small sauce pan.

Add flour, salt and pepper, cook until bubbly.

Add milk and stir constantly until sauce thickens.

Pour sauce into skillet with cooked chicken, mix together.

Serve over hot rice.

Yield: 4 servings

*Recipe was tested using fat-free milk

Nut-Crusted Baked Fish

3 tablespoons GF dry bread crumbs*
3 tablespoons finely chopped pecans
¼ teaspoon Italian seasoning
¼ teaspoon salt
Dash pepper
3 tablespoons GF all-purpose flour
3 tablespoons milk**
½ pound fish fillets

Preheat oven to 400°.

In a shallow bowl, combine the bread crumbs, pecans, Italian seasoning, salt and pepper.

Place the flour in a second shallow bowl and the milk in a third bowl.

Dredge fish fillets in flour, dip in milk, then coat with the crumb mixture.

Bake for 10–15 minutes or until fish flakes easily with fork.

Yield: 2 servings

*See Helpful Hints
**Recipe was tested using fat-free milk

"I loved the nutty flavor and this is the first baked fish I've had. It was excellent!"
–Barb Lawrenz

Saucy Chicken

4 boneless and skinless chicken breasts
1 large onion, chopped
2 tablespoons olive oil
3 tablespoons granulated sugar
3 tablespoons ketchup
2 tablespoons soy sauce
2 tablespoons lemon juice
⅛ teaspoon pepper
2 tablespoons water
1 tablespoon cornstarch

Sauté onion in olive oil until tender.

In a small bowl, mix next five ingredients together.

Add to onion and cook until mixture boils. Add chicken breasts and simmer 25–30 minutes.

Remove chicken from sauce.

Mix water and cornstarch together and add to sauce, cooking until thick.

Serve hot sauce over chicken breasts.

Yield: 4 servings

Baked Almond Chicken

½ cup GF all-purpose flour
⅓ cup (5 ⅓ tablespoons) plus 1 tablespoon butter, melted, *divided*
1 teaspoon celery salt
1 teaspoon paprika
½ teaspoon salt
½ teaspoon dried oregano
¼ teaspoon pepper
6 boneless chicken breast halves
1 ½ cup whipping cream
⅓ cup GF dry bread crumbs*
¾ cup sliced almonds, toasted
Hot cooked GF pasta

Preheat oven to 350°. Grease shallow 3-qt. baking dish.

Place flour in a shallow bowl.

Combine ⅓ cup butter and next five ingredients in another bowl.

Coat chicken with flour, then dip in butter mixture. Arrange in prepared baking dish. Pour cream around chicken.

Bake, uncovered, for 45 minutes.

Combine bread crumbs and remaining butter; sprinkle over chicken. Top with almonds.

Bake, uncovered, for 5–8 minutes or until golden brown.

Serve over pasta.

Yield: 6 servings

*See Helpful Hints

Baked Cavatini

2 ½ cups GF brown rice penne pasta
1 pound lean ground beef
½ cup chopped onion
2 cloves garlic, minced
1 teaspoon Italian seasoning
⅛ teaspoon pepper
1 15-ounce can tomato sauce
1 13-ounce jar spaghetti sauce
1 cup shredded mozzarella cheese

Preheat oven to 375°.

Cook pasta according to package directions.

While pasta is cooking, brown ground beef, onions and garlic in skillet. After meat is browned, add next four ingredients; mix well.

Drain pasta and add to meat mixture.

Place in 13-in. x 9-in. baking dish and cover with mozzarella cheese.

Bake covered for 25–35 minutes, then uncovered for 10–15 minutes.

Yield: 4–6 servings

Oven Baked Chicken Parmesan

4 boneless, skinless chicken breasts
1 egg, slightly beaten
¾ cup GF dry bread crumbs*
1 teaspoon Italian seasoning
1 jar (26-28 oz.) pasta sauce
1 cup shredded mozzarella cheese (about 4 oz.)
Gluten-free pasta

Preheat oven to 400°.

Combine bread crumbs with Italian seasoning.

Rinse chicken breasts under cold water. Pound each breast to ¼–½ inch thickness.

Dip chicken in egg, then bread crumbs. Arrange chicken in 13x9 inch baking dish.

Bake chicken uncovered for 20 minutes.

While chicken is baking, cook pasta according to package directions.

Pour pasta sauce over chicken, then top with cheese.

Bake 10 minutes longer or until chicken is no longer pink. Serve over cooked pasta.

Yield: 4 servings

*See Helpful Hints

Baked Parmesan Fish

2 tablespoons GF dry bread crumbs*
1 tablespoon Parmesan cheese
2 teaspoons paprika
1 teaspoon dried basil
1 pound perch or fish fillets of your choice
1 ½ tablespoon butter, melted

In a shallow bowl, combine the first four ingredients.

In a separate small bowl, melt butter.

Dip fish fillets in melted butter, then dip into the crumb mixture. Place in a greased baking pan.

Bake, uncovered at 400° for 12–15 minutes or until fish flakes easily with fork.

Yield: 2 servings

*See Helpful Hints

Lots of Beef

1 boneless bottom round roast (4–5 pounds), cut into ¾ inch cubes
1 large onion, chopped
4 garlic cloves, minced
2 tablespoons olive oil
1 ½ cup water
1 teaspoon salt
½ teaspoon pepper

In a Dutch oven, cook beef, onions and garlic in oil until beef is brown; drain.

Stir in water, salt and pepper.

Bring to a boil.

Reduce heat; cover and simmer for 1¾–2 hours or until meat is tender.

Cool. Divide beef and cooking liquid between 3–4 freezer containers, cover and freeze.

May be frozen for up to 3 months.

Crispy Herbed Coating

½ cup GF corn meal
¼ cup GF all-purpose flour
2 tablespoons grated Parmesan cheese
1 ½ teaspoons Italian seasoning
¼ teaspoon garlic salt
¼ teaspoon pepper
½ cup milk*
3 tablespoons melted butter
4–5 boneless chicken breasts or 4–5 fish fillets

Preheat oven to 400°.

In a shallow bowl, combine first six ingredients.

Put milk in separate bowl.

Dip fish or chicken into milk; coat with corn meal mixture.

Place meat in 9-in. x 13-in. baking pan.

Drizzle butter over meat.

Bake fish for 10–15 minutes, chicken for 20–25 minutes, or until golden brown.

Yield: 4–5 servings

*Recipe was tested using fat-free milk

This coating is great on chicken or fish!

BBQ Meatballs

¾ cup quinoa flakes
1 can (5 ounces) evaporated milk
1 egg, beaten
¾ teaspoon salt
¾ teaspoon chili powder
¼ teaspoon garlic powder or 1–2 garlic cloves, minced
¼ teaspoon pepper
1 ¼ pounds lean ground beef

SAUCE:
1 ½ cups ketchup
⅔ cup packed brown sugar
¼ cup chopped onion
¼ teaspoon garlic powder

Preheat oven to 350°.

In a large bowl, combine the first seven ingredients.

Crumble beef over mixture and mix well. Shape into 1 ½ inch balls. Place 1 inch apart in ungreased 13- in. x 9-in. x 2-in. baking dish.

Combine the sauce ingredients; pour over meatballs.

Bake, uncovered for 45–50 minutes or until meat is no longer pink and a meat thermometer reads 160°.

These freeze well.

To reheat frozen meatballs:

Thaw in the refrigerator or remove from the freezer 30 minutes before baking.

Bake, uncovered, at 350° for 20–25 minutes or until heated through.

Meatballs and Sauce

2 eggs, beaten
½ cup GF dry bread crumbs*
¼ cup grated Parmesan or Romano cheese
2 tablespoons minced fresh parsley
2 garlic cloves, minced
⅛ teaspoon pepper
1 pound ground beef
2 tablespoons olive oil

SAUCE:
2–3 garlic cloves, minced
1 tablespoon olive oil
2 cans (28 ounce each) crushed tomatoes in puree
2–3 cups water, *divided*
1 can (8 ounce) tomato sauce
1 can (6 ounce) tomato paste
½ cup minced fresh parsley
¼ cup grated Parmesan or Romano cheese
1 tablespoon dried basil
2–3 teaspoons brown sugar
½ teaspoon salt
¼ teaspoon pepper

In a large bowl, combine the first six ingredients.

Crumble beef over mixture and mix well.

Shape into 12 meatballs.

In a large skillet, brown meatballs in oil on all sides; drain.

In a Dutch oven, sauté garlic in oil for 1 minute. Stir in the tomatoes, 2 cups water and the next six ingredients; bring to a boil.

Reduce heat; carefully add meatballs.

Cover and simmer for 3 hours, adding more water if needed to achieve desired consistency.

Season with salt and pepper.

Yield: 6 servings

*See Helpful Hints

Thick Beef Stew

1 portion Lots of Beef* (see page 102), thawed
3 medium red potatoes, cubed
1 ¼ cups water
1 to 1 ½ teaspoons dried oregano
1 teaspoon salt
1 cup frozen green beans
1 cup sliced carrots
1 tablespoon cornstarch
2 tablespoons water

In a saucepan, combine the beef, potatoes, carrots, water, oregano and salt.

Bring to a boil.

Reduce heat; cover and simmer for 10–15 minutes or until potatoes are tender.

Add green beans and heat through.

Combine cornstarch and water until smooth; gradually add to beef mixture.

Bring to a boil; cook and stir for 2 minutes or until thickened and bubbly.

Yield: 4 servings

*2 cups of cubed cooked beef and ½ cup beef broth may be substituted.

Lindy's note:
I usually let this simmer on the stove for 1–2 hours before adding the water and cornstarch.

Mini Cheddar Meat Loaves

1 egg, lightly beaten
¼ cup GF dry bread crumbs*
2 tablespoons ketchup
1 tablespoon chopped onion
½ pound lean ground beef

TOPPING:
4 teaspoons ketchup
4 tablespoons shredded cheddar cheese

Preheat oven to 400°. Coat four muffin cups with nonstick cooking spray.

In a large bowl, combine the first four ingredients.

Crumble beef over mixture and mix well.

Fill prepared muffin cups three-fourths full with meat mixture. Spread ketchup over loaves.

Bake for 15 minutes.

Sprinkle with cheese. Bake 5 minutes longer or until a meat thermometer reads 160°.

Let stand 5 minutes before removing from muffin cups.

Yield: 2 servings

*See Helpful Hints

Barbecued Chicken 'n Rice

⅓ cup chopped onion
2 tablespoons chopped celery
1 tablespoon olive oil
1 cup ketchup
⅓ cup packed brown sugar
3 tablespoons apple cider vinegar
2 tablespoons water
1 tablespoon Worcestershire sauce
2 teaspoons prepared mustard
½ teaspoon salt
2 garlic cloves, minced
1 ½ cups quick cooking brown rice
1 ¼ cups chicken broth
4 boneless skinless chicken breasts

In a saucepan, sauté onion and celery in olive oil until tender. Add the next eight ingredients.

Simmer, uncovered, for 20–30 minutes, stirring occasionally.

Preheat oven to 400°. Grease a 13-in. x 9-in. x 2-in. baking dish.

Meanwhile, combine rice and broth in prepared baking dish.

Top with chicken and barbecue sauce.

Bake, uncovered for 25–30 minutes or until the rice is tender and meat juices run clear.

Yield: 4 servings

"Man does not live on bread alone, but on every word that comes from the mouth of God."
-The Bible

Gluten-Free Soups & Sandwiches

109
soups & sandwiches

Chicken Pita Sandwiches

1 package (8 ounces) whipped cream cheese
3 tablespoons milk
1 tablespoon lemon juice
2 cups cubed, cooked chicken
2 tablespoons snipped chives
1 celery stalk, chopped
1 teaspoon ground mustard
¼ teaspoon dried thyme
½ teaspoon salt
⅛ teaspoon pepper
¼ cup chopped walnuts
3 large GF pita breads*, halved and split open to form pocket

In a mixing bowl, beat cream cheese, milk and lemon juice until smooth.

Stir in the chicken and remaining ingredients.

Spoon about ½ cup filling into each pita half.

Sprinkle additional chopped nuts on top if desired.

Yield: 3–6 servings

*See Helpful Hints

Parmesan Corn Chowder

2 cups water
2 cups diced peeled potatoes
½ cup sliced carrots
½ cup sliced celery
¼ cup chopped onion
¼ cup butter
¼ cup GF all-purpose flour
1 teaspoon salt
½ teaspoon pepper
2 cups milk*
1 can (14 ¾ ounces) cream-style corn
1 ½ cups (6 ounces) shredded Parmesan cheese

In a large saucepan, combine the first five ingredients; bring to a boil.

Reduce heat; cover and simmer for 12–15 minutes or until vegetables are tender (do not drain).

Meanwhile, in a small saucepan, melt butter, stir in flour, salt and pepper until smooth; gradually stir in milk.

Bring to a boil; cook and stir for 2 minutes or until thickened.

Stir into the vegetable mixture. Add corn and Parmesan cheese.

Cook 10 minutes longer or until heated through.

Yield: 7 servings

*Recipe was tested using fat-free milk

Fruit & Turkey Panini

8 slices GF bread*
8 slices deli turkey
1 small apple, peeled, cored and thinly sliced
4 slices cheddar cheese (or cheese of choice)
4 tablespoons cranberry sauce
Olive oil

Spread one side of each bread slice with olive oil and lay the bread oil-side down on the work surface.

Place the turkey, apple slices, cheese and cranberry sauce on the top of one slice of bread.

Put the second slice of bread on the top, oil side up.

Grill using sandwich maker or grill in skillet on medium heat and cook the sandwich on each side about 3–4 minutes until golden brown.

Yield: 4 servings

*See Helpful Hints

> "Man, that was really good! Can I have the recipe for this?"
> -Joe Eckstein

Delightful Chicken Pitas

½ cup light mayonnaise
1 tablespoon honey
2 cups shredded cooked chicken
1 cup red grapes, halved
½ cup chopped pecans
1 tablespoon finely chopped onion
4 GF pita breads*, halved and split open to form pocket
Lettuce leaves

In a bowl, combine mayonnaise and honey.

Stir in the chicken, grapes, pecans and onion.

Line pita halves with lettuce; fill with chicken mixture.

Yield: 4 servings

*See Helpful Hints

Best Potato Soup

6 slices turkey bacon
1 can (14 ½ ounces) chicken broth
3 cups cubed peeled potatoes
2 medium carrots, grated
½ cup chopped onion
1 tablespoon dried parsley flakes
½ teaspoon celery seed
½ teaspoon salt
½ teaspoon pepper
3 tablespoons GF all-purpose flour
3 cups milk*
8 ounces grated cheddar cheese (sharp or mild)

Cook bacon in microwave until crisp. Place next eight ingredients in a large saucepan. Cover and simmer until potatoes are tender, about 15 minutes.

Using a jar or cup with tight-fitting lid, combine flour and 1 cup milk, seal jar and shake until smooth; add to soup along with remaining 2 cups of milk.

Bring to boil; boil and stir for 2 minutes. Add cheese; stir until cheese is melted and the soup is heated through. Garnish with crumbled bacon and if desired, additional grated cheese.

Yield: 8 servings (2 quarts)

*Recipe was tested using fat-free milk.

Italian Vegetable Soup

2 cans (14 ½ ounce each) organic chicken broth
1 medium potato, cubed
1 medium onion, chopped
1 medium carrot, chopped
1 celery rib, chopped
½ cup frozen green beans
1 bay leaf
Liberal amount of Italian seasoning
⅛ teaspoon pepper
½ cup GF small shell pasta, cooked and drained
1 can (14 ½ ounces) diced tomatoes, undrained

In a large saucepan, combine the first nine ingredients.

Bring to a boil.

Reduce heat; cover and simmer for 15–20 minutes or until vegetables are crisp-tender.

Add the pasta and tomatoes; heat through.

Discard bay leaf before serving.

Yield: 6 servings

Bountiful Harvest Pizza

3 cups shredded zucchini
3 eggs, lightly beaten
⅓ cup GF all-purpose flour
½ teaspoon salt
¼ teaspoon xanthan gum
2 cups (8 ounces) shredded mozzarella cheese
2 small tomatoes, thinly sliced
½ cup chopped onion
2 teaspoons Italian seasoning
½ cup fresh basil, cut in strips
3 tablespoons shredded Parmesan cheese

Preheat oven to 450°. Grease bottom of 12-in. pizza pan.

In a large bowl, combine zucchini and eggs. Whisk together the next three ingredients, stir into zucchini mixture.

Spread zucchini mixture onto the bottom of prepared pan. Bake for 8 minutes.

Remove pan from oven and reduce heat to 350°.

Sprinkle zucchini crust with mozzarella cheese. Place tomatoes and onion over cheese. Sprinkle with Italian seasoning, basil and Parmesan cheese.

Bake for 15-20 minutes or until onion is tender and cheese is melted.

Yield: 6–8 slices

Toasted Cheese and Turkey

8 slices GF bread*
Mayonnaise (optional)
6 ounces thinly sliced deli turkey
8 thin slices sharp cheddar cheese
4 tomato slices (optional)
¼ cup olive oil

Spread each slice of bread with mayonnaise (optional).

Layer four slices with cheese, turkey, tomato (optional), and cheese.

Cover with remaining bread slices.

Brush outside of each sandwich with olive oil.

In a skillet, griddle or sandwich maker, grill over medium heat until bread is lightly browned and cheese is melted.

Yield: 4 servings

*See Helpful Hints

Glossary

Baking Powder—non-aluminized or aluminized: Baking powder is a dry chemical leavening agent used to increase the volume and lighten the texture of baked goods such as muffins, cakes, scones, and biscuits. Baking powders are available both with and without aluminum compounds. Some people prefer not to use baking powder with aluminum because they believe it gives food a vaguely metallic taste.

Butter Flavoring: A flavoring added to enhance the butter taste in a baked item. Can be found in the spice section of your local grocery store.

Butter Measures: ¼ cup = ½ stick, ½ cup = 1 stick, ¾ cup = 1 ½ sticks, 1 cup = 2 sticks

Chives snipped: Chives belong to the same family as onions, leeks, and garlic. Chives taste like a sweeter, milder version of an onion. Using kitchen scissors, cut the leaves into small pieces and use as garnish, or flavoring on meats, vegetables, etc.

Cooked Pumpkin: Same as canned pumpkin, can usually be found in baking isle with pie fillings.

Cornstarch: Cornstarch is a thickening agent that is the bland, gluten-free alternative to flour for frying and for sauces and gravies. Use it in cakes, cookies, pies, and a host of other sweet goods. Many cooks prefer using cornstarch as it imparts no additional flavor to foods.

Cream (together): Means to beat together in the same bowl, typically butter or cream cheese with sugar. Bring the butter or cream cheese to room temperature and beat them with a hand or stand mixer until well blended and smooth.

Cut in: Means to incorporate cold butter or shortening into flour. After cutting butter into cubes, place butter into flour mixture. Use a pastry blender or two knives to push/cut the butter into the flour. Continue this process until desired consistency is achieved—usually coarse crumbs.

Double Boiler: A large pan containing hot water, into which other smaller pans are set in order to cook food at low heat (below 100°C/212°F), or to keep food warm.

Divided: Refers to saving a portion of that ingredient/mixture to be used at separate times in the recipe.

Eggs (separated): Use two bowls or cups. Gently crack the egg on a flat surface as close to the middle of the egg as possible. Working over one bowl, use your thumbs to gently pry the egg shell apart. Let the egg yolk settle in one half of the egg shell while the egg whites run off the sides of the shell into the bowl. Gently transfer the yolk back and forth between the egg shell halves, letting as much egg white as possible to drip into the bowl. Try not to break the egg yolk. Place egg yolk in second bowl.

Fold in: To gently combine lighter mixtures with heavier ones, usually using a metal spoon or spatula in a cutting or slicing "J" movement while slightly lifting the utensil.

Ginger (diced-crystallized): The dried root of the ginger plant. It looks like dried pineapple. This product is not carried in all stores. Ask your grocer if they have it or can carry it.

Gluten-Free All-Purpose Baking Flour: This is a relatively new blend of several flours that help to replace traditional wheat flour for baking. It is higher in protein because of the amount of bean flours used in the blend. It contains garbanzo flour, potato starch, tapioca flour, sorghum flour, and fava flour. Nearly all recipes in *Lindy's Gluten-free Goodies and More!* use Bob's Red Mill Gluten-Free All-Purpose Baking Flour.

Granulated sugar: Ordinary white sugar, for domestic use, having a relatively large crystal size.

Knead: The act of pressing down on dough with the heels of both your palms and pushing it forward to stretch it, then pulling it back toward you.

Parchment Paper: Baking paper that helps keep baked items from sticking. It makes the baked good easier to remove from a baking pan.

Scant teaspoon: Not quite full teaspoon.

Slightly beaten: Use a fork or whisk to beat eggs just until the yolks and whites are blended.

Stir in: Use a spatula to blend ingredients in a circular motion until mixed together.

Vanilla Extract: A liquid—technically a tincture—used in cooking, prepared by soaking vanilla beans in alcohol.

Whisk together: Use a wired loop instrument with a handle (a whisk) to blend ingredients smooth or to incorporate air into a mixture.

Xanthan gum: Since the gluten found in wheat must be omitted, xanthan gum is used to give the dough or batter a "stickiness" that would otherwise be achieved with the gluten.

Order a Copy of This Book

Would you like a copy of this book for yourself or a loved one?

Order online:

www.GlutenFreeByLindy.com
Amazon.com and BarnesandNoble.com

Order through your local bookstore:

Take this number to your local bookstore: ISBN 978-0-9852577-3-6

Look for Lindy's next cookbook, *OMG, It's Gluten-Free!*